Also by María Fernández-Toro:

Training learners for self-instruction

The Centre for Information on
Language Teaching and Research
provides a complete range of services
for language professionals in every
stage and sector of education, and in
business, in support of its brief to
promote Britain's foreign language
capability.

CILT is a registered charity, supported
by Central Government grants. CILT
is based in Covent Garden, London,
and its services are delivered through
a national collaborative network of
regional Comenius Centres in
England, the National Comenius
Centre of Wales, Scottish CILT and
Northern Ireland CILT.

CILT Publications are available through
all good booksellers or directly from:

Central Books, 99 Wallis Rd,
London E9 5LN.
Tel: 020 8986 4854. Fax: 020 8533 5821.

DIY

techniques

for

language

learners

María Fernández-Toro and
Francis R Jones

Centre for Information
on Language Teaching and Research

The views expressed in this publication are the authors' and do not necessarily represent those of CILT.

Acknowledgements

The authors wish to thank all their colleagues from the Language Centre, University of Newcastle upon Tyne, and particularly Andrea Wilczynski, for piloting the materials and providing valuable feedback. Very many thanks too to David Westgate for his indefatigably positive and astute feedback on the PhD project that was one of the sources of this handbook, and to Elspeth Broady and Richard Johnstone for their feedback and encouragement about and after the project. We also would like to thank our spouses and relatives, especially Jim Bateman, Alexandre Fernández and Audrey Holt, for their support and feedback. Last but by no means least, a very warm thank-you to the many self-instructed learners who talked about their experiences and gave their invaluable advice on how to make independent learning work, and to the hundreds of students who tried out the techniques and helped us improve them over the last few years. We hope the book will contribute to making language learning an enjoyable and fruitful experience for many more learners to come.

First published 2001 by the Centre for Information on Language Teaching and Research (CILT), 20 Bedfordbury, London WC2N 4LB

ISBN 1 902031 46 6

2005 2004 2003 2002 2001 / 10 9 8 7 6 5 4 3 2 1

A catalogue record for this book is available from the British Library

Printed in Great Britain by Copyprint UK Ltd

CILT Publications are available from: **Central Books**, 99 Wallis Rd, London E9 5LN. Tel: 020 8986 4854. Fax: 020 8533 5821. Book trade representation (UK and Ireland): **Broadcast Book Services,** Charter House, 27a London Road, Croydon CR0 2RE. Tel: 020 8681 8949. Fax: 020 8688 0615.

contents

part

1

Laying the ground

1 Introduction

Who is this book for?

KEY TERMS

Teach-yourself = self-instruction = learning a language without a class.

Independent learning = taking responsibility for your own learning; planning and using various learning methods (wholly or partly self-instruction-based) to suit your own situation and needs.

Self-access = working on tasks by yourself as part of a taught course, usually in a self-access centre (see below).

Self-access centre = open access centre = open learning centre = resource centre = an area in a school, college or university with self-instruction materials, cassette players, etc.

A language centre = a college or university department that usually runs classes as well as having a self-access centre.

This book aims to give practical information, ideas and techniques to help people who are teaching themselves a foreign language. They may be learning at home, or in a school, college or university language centre. They may be using a coursebook with cassettes or videos, or they may be using real-life reading and listening materials and talking with native speakers. Some may be learning completely solo, others may be learning together with family or friends, and yet others may have a teacher or language centre advisor to guide them. Some may be teaching themselves because there is no class available or they find classwork too restrictive, and others may be combining teach-yourself work with a taught course.

But what links all these learners is that they are learning independently – in other words, that they have taken responsibility for their own learning. If **you** are an independent language learner – whether you are learning for fun or holidays, for business or work, or as part of your studies – this book is for you.

If you are a language teacher, this book is also aimed at you. The ideas listed here can be suggested to your students – or, better still, the training activities can be carried out in the classroom, helping them to build up a life-long toolkit for learning languages.

Alternatively, you may be a language-learning advisor, or you may be running a self-access centre in a school, college or university. For you too, this book should form a valuable resource: both to have on the shelves for learners to refer to directly, and to use as a source of advice to give to learners via counselling sessions, posters, handbooks, etc.

The ideas and techniques we provide here are tried and tested. Many come from our own experience as learners, and as teachers and learning trainers working with adults. Others come from learners themselves: many of the techniques in this book, in fact, come from interviews with a large number of adult learners.

This does not mean, by the way, that only adults can benefit from this book. Most of the activities and techniques can also be used by teenagers, and many could be adapted for use by younger learners.

Aims of this book

KEY TERMS

Language skills = what you do with the language (reading, writing, listening, speaking, etc).

Language areas = what the language is made up of (vocabulary, grammar, etc).

Learning style = your personal, preferred approach to learning a language.

Learning strategies = techniques you use to help yourself learn (e.g. using a dictionary, trying to meet native speakers, etc).

Teach-yourself package = a complete self-instruction course, usually consisting of a coursebook and very often a cassette; it may contain other components, such as a CD-ROM or video.

This book has two key aims. The first is to give you practical information about self-instructed learning – that is, about:

- the different self-instructed learning options that exist;
- what options and activities are most likely to suit you and your learning needs;
- what learning a skill or language area actually involves.

Armed with this information, you will be able to learn more effectively, tailoring your learning to fit:

- your own learning style (for instance, whether you prefer to learn by studying or by communicating with people);
- your own needs (for instance, whether you are learning a language for business or for holidays);
- the skill or language area you are working on (working on listening, for instance, requires different strategies from reading).

Our second and more important aim is to build on this foundation by giving practical language-learning advice. This advice is of two types. Part 1 contains general advice – how to make the best of your learning personality, how to set up your own learning programme, how to choose and use published teach-yourself packages, and so on. Part 2 describes ready-to-use 'DIY techniques' for a wide range of language-learning tasks and skills. These techniques can be used with any foreign language, and most can be used at any proficiency level (beginner, intermediate or advanced). With each technique, we tell you:

- what it is useful for;
- how to use it;
- how to get feedback on whether you are using the language correctly or whether you are making progress;
- additional tips and variations.

How to use this book

Because **Part 1** gives a general grounding in principles of independent learning – plus a lot of useful advice – we recommend that you start by reading it through. If you wish to discover your own language learning profile, a series of questionnaires is provided in Chapter 5. Some of the advice given in **Part 1** refers to particular learning profiles.

In **Part 2**, the chapters – *Vocabulary, Grammar, Reading, Listening, Writing, Speaking* – stand independently. Each has two sections: an introduction to the language area or skill in question ('What does learning X involve?'), and a list of 'DIY techniques' to improve the area or skill.

There are three ways in which **Part 2** can be used:

1 Go directly to the chapter that interests you most (e.g. *Speaking*), read through the full chapter, and choose which techniques to try out.

2 Go to Sections 5.4–5.9 of Chapter 5 (*Diagnostic questionnaires*). These sections contain checklists of 'typical problems' related to vocabulary, grammar, reading, listening, writing and speaking.

Each problem is matched to a set of recommended 'DIY solutions' – either strategies described in **Part 1** or DIY techniques described in **Part 2.** Then look up the strategies and/or techniques recommended, read them through, and try them out in your own language learning. However, we also recommend that you find time to read the first section of any **Part 2** chapters to which you are directed (entitled 'What does learning X involve?'), as this will give you valuable background information about the language areas or skills in question.

3   Refer to the full alphabetical listing of DIY techniques at the end of the book (p137).

The symbol ▶ is used throughout the book for cross-referencing purposes. It normally points the reader to specific DIY techniques that are fully described in Part 2. For instance, ▶ **[G5]** *Self-transcript* indicates that 'Self-transcript' is the fifth technique in the Grammar chapter (indicated by **[G5]** in square brackets).

Independent learning: benefits, barriers and solutions

The term 'independent learning' covers a wide range of learning modes. Some learners may decide to study completely solo, or they may follow a class while working through a teach-yourself course in their free time. Others may rely mainly on a taught course with only a small self-instruction element – taking French classes but also working in the self-access centre once a week, for example.

Independent learning, of course, is not all plain sailing. Learning a complex skill – be it learning to speak French, to drive a truck, or to knit a Fair-Isle jumper – takes time and effort, and the more independently you learn, the more you are reliant on your own motivation and language-learning skills. It would be dishonest of us to deny this – but it is also worth stressing that independent learning has real advantages, which learners would miss out on if they relied simply on a teacher and a class. In this section, we discuss the benefits of teaching yourself a foreign language, look realistically at the barriers that can get in the way, and look at possible ways of getting round these barriers.

KEY TERMS

Proficiency (level) = command = how well you know a language:

- **Elementary** = having a basic stock of words, phrases and grammar – enough to survive as a tourist, say

- **Intermediate** = able to get by in a rough-and-ready way in most situations

- **Advanced** = able to understand and express virtually everything

Solo learning: *'I did it my way'*, or *'The long and winding road'*?

One benefit of working on your own is that learning is tailored just for you: it is you who decide what and how to learn. On the other hand, you stand a higher risk of running out of motivation, and even giving up. It can also be more difficult to get speaking practice and feedback on progress. Teaching yourself, however, does not rule out joining a class (and vice versa). A class gives a regular framework which makes it more difficult to simply forget to keep learning, a teacher can supply feedback, and if you get on well with your fellow learners, seeing them gives an extra reason for coming to class.

Research shows that the best balance of learning methods depends on your proficiency level: where you are now, and how far you want to get. If you are a beginner or elementary-level learner, using a teach-yourself course is an excellent way of getting a quick smattering of a language; but joining a class is best if you want to get further in the language, because the extra motivation helps fight the temptation to drop out once the initial enthusiasm wears off. If you already have an intermediate 'get-by' ability in speaking and reading, however, classwork can feel increasingly restrictive: then, adding a self-taught element gives a vital boost to your learning, for you are learning what you want in ways that you enjoy. At this stage, research shows that you don't need to keep going to a class (especially if you are in the foreign country) – but some learners like to do so for the social contact it brings, or to get teacher's feedback on speaking and writing. We will return to the issue of fitting learning resources to your proficiency level in Chapter 3 (▶ 'Learning means', p16).

A matter of timing

Another benefit of working on your own is that you can put in more hours than if you were just following a class, and at times that suit you – which means you can learn faster. The problem is that, with the busy lives we lead today, it's easy to put off language learning till tomorrow … or the day after … or the day after that … Experienced self-instructed learners say that the solution is to set up a daily working routine, and stick to it. This is a topic we will come back to in Chapter 3 (▶ 'Time resources', p18).

Finding the tools

A third benefit of teaching yourself is that you can choose your own learning materials to suit your own needs and learning style. A problem for some learners, however, might be that they do not know what materials are available and where to get them from. Solutions to this problem are provided in Chapter 3 (▶ 'Learning means', p16), where we give tips on what learning resources to use and how to get hold of them.

Now, in fact, it is time to turn to the main purpose of this book: to help you become a more effective independent learner. In the rest of Part 1 we give advice on general approaches to self-instruction; and in Part 2 we present DIY techniques for specific language skills and areas.

2

You as a learner

KEY TERMS

Self-instruction aptitude = a 'gift' for teaching yourself a language. Research shows that it contains both the ability to make sense of a new foreign language and the discipline to keep learning.

The first question in any overview of how to learn is: who is doing the learning? In this chapter we look at differences between learners – in terms of learning style, self-instruction aptitude, language learning experience, and proficiency level in the language in question – and at how these differences can affect the learning process. We also give some learning tips connected with these individual differences.

Learning style

What is learning style?

Your learning style shows your preferred way of learning new skills. There are many learning-style differences between learners: some learners are visual (i.e. they like learning by seeing) and some are verbal (i.e. they like learning by hearing); some learners are holistic (i.e. they like going for the whole picture) whereas others prefer to focus on details, etc. The learning-style difference which seems to be most important for foreign language learning, however, is that between 'experiential' and 'studial' learners. This can be seen as a scale:

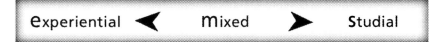

experiential ◀ mixed ▶ Studial

e If you are more **experiential**, you prefer to learn through hands-on experience. This means that you like to learn languages by reading, listening and talking to others, by simply using the language in the foreign country and with native speakers, even if communicating is a rough-and-ready business at first. You probably find textbook exercises dry, however, and textbook language explanations hard to understand.

s If you are more **studial**, you prefer to learn by studying how things work. This means that you like to learn languages by reading grammar explanations, memorising word-lists and doing language exercises. You prefer not to try communicating with people until you have built up enough knowledge to feel confident.

m Many (if not most) people, however, have a **mixed** learning style, using sometimes experiential and sometimes studial learning strategies. The important thing is that no learning style is better than another: any point on the learning-style scale can lead to mastery of a foreign language in the end.

If you are not sure what you are, first use the Learning style questionnaire in Chapter 5 (p35). If you feel you already know your learning style, read on: if you see yourself as an experiential learner, read 'Experiential strengths and challenges' below; if you see yourself as a studial learner, read 'Studial strengths and challenges' (p9) below; if you see yourself as a mixed-style learner, read both sections.

Experiential strengths and challenges

The typical experiential learner has certain strengths, but also faces certain 'challenges', i.e. obstacles to learning, or learning activities which go against the grain. Below we list the main strengths and challenges (•), and give learning tips (✔) connected with each.

Experiential strengths

- You probably like learning by communicating with people:
  - ✔ For ideas on how to meet people and use them to help your language learning, see Chapter 4 below (▶ 'People as a learning resource', p23).
  - ✔ Don't just chat: give yourself a learning aim. For example, try to turn the topic to a vocabulary area you have just been learning.
  - ✔ Don't just speak – write to people as well! See Chapter 10 for tips.
- You probably like 'having a go' in conversations, even if you make mistakes:
  - ✔ This is an excellent way of learning. Don't worry about the mistakes: you will become more accurate with practice!
- Talking with other people gives you good feedback on how you are progressing:
  - ✔ For feedback ideas if you have no-one to speak to, see Chapter 4 below (▶ 'Getting feedback', p31).
- You might well be good at 'picking up' pronunciation:
  - ✔ If you feel you're not, or if you want to work actively on your pronunciation, see Chapter 11 below.

Experiential challenges

- You probably find coursebook language explanations hard to understand:
  - ✔ Don't worry: learning language rules 'by feel' is just as good as learning by rote.
  - ✔ Try targeting certain grammar forms in conversation (for instance, past verb endings): listen for what people use, and try out these forms when it is your turn to speak.
- If you know one language (e.g. German) and then start on a second language in the same family (e.g. Dutch), you may feel that the first 'interferes' with the second:
  - ✔ See Chapter 4 (▶ 'Using related languages', p32) for advice.
- You may feel the language you're learning is 'difficult':
  - ✔ Remember that no language is any more difficult than any other. Ask any native-speaker toddler!
  - ✔ Much of what seems difficult is probably just unfamiliar. With practice, things will get easier.

✔ Every language (even English!) has one or two nasty areas that foreigners find very hard. Native speakers will understand this, and will not be upset by foreigners' mistakes in these areas.

Studial strengths and challenges

Similarly, the typical studial learner has certain strengths, but also faces certain 'challenges', i.e. obstacles to learning, or learning activities which go against the grain. Below we list the main strengths and challenges (●), and give tips (✔) connected with each.

Studial strengths

● You probably like to understand how a piece of language works before trying it out:

   ✔ See this as a strength, not a weakness!

   ✔ In the foreign country, have a pocket dictionary (and maybe a grammar) on you at all times. If you have a difficult encounter coming up (e.g. booking places on an excursion), look up the key words a few minutes before and practise what you're going to say.

● You are probably quite good at coping with language explanations and learning grammar tables:

   ✔ These give an excellent base. But don't forget practice activities: if you don't use it, you lose it!

   ✔ Re-read explanations and re-learn tables at a later date, once you have experience of using and understanding the words and grammar. You'll remember them much more easily then.

● You are probably quite good at using similarities between languages to help you learn:

   ✔ See Chapter 4 (▶ 'Using related languages', p32) for more tips.

● 'Difficult' languages probably don't worry you:

   ✔ Why not try a really exotic language? It might be fun!

Studial challenges

● If you're just beginning a foreign language, you may find native speakers hard to understand or too daunting to speak to in their language – or they may not appreciate your efforts:

   ✔ Try some of the activities in Chapter 11 that don't involve native speakers.

   ✔ Take a trip to the foreign country as soon as possible, and try to do things (like shopping) on your own, preferably in places where few people speak English. Once you see how far even a few words can get you, it will boost your confidence.

   ✔ As your knowledge of the language increases, communication will get easier, and people will be more appreciative of your efforts.

● Native speakers may seem difficult to find:

   ✔ See Chapter 4 (▶ 'People as a learning resource', p23) for how to get in touch with native speakers, or to find other people you can talk and/or work with.

● You may find pronunciation difficult:

   ✔ Regular work with cassettes (e.g. repetition) pays big dividends here: try it! See Chapter 11 for more activity ideas.

✔ In the meantime, don't worry: comprehensibility is more important than native-like pronunciation.

- It may seem difficult to get feedback on your progress:
  ✔ See Chapter 4 (▶ 'Getting feedback', p31) for tips.

Self-instruction aptitude

What is aptitude?

Whereas learning style shows **how** you learn, aptitude shows **how well** you learn. Though language aptitude – a 'gift for languages' – is not as big an influence on foreign language learning as many people think (it is less important than motivation, say), having good aptitude can certainly boost your learning speed. Our research shows that 'self-instruction aptitude' (i.e. language aptitude as applied to self-instruction) consists of two key elements:

- a **sensitivity to language** in general, including one's own;
- **self-discipline and organisation skills**: the ability to find time to learn, to set up a regular working routine, and not to give up once the initial enthusiasm wears off.

How does your aptitude affect your learning?

Before going ahead, we recommend that you do the Self-instruction aptitude questionnaire in Chapter 5 (p37), as modesty may lead you to under-rate yourself. Once you have an idea of your language aptitude, read the appropriate box below.

High self-instruction aptitude

You have excellent language sensitivity and self-discipline. If other conditions (such as motivation and learning resources) are also favourable, this should give you a strong chance of success in your foreign language.

- Language sensitivity, however, is no more than a foundation for language learning, so boost your learning power even further by trying out activities in this book that are new to you.
- As for self-discipline, read Chapter 3: some tips may be new to you.

Medium self-instruction aptitude

You have reasonable-to-good language sensitivity and/or self-discipline, which will increase your chances of success in foreign language learning.

- Even good language sensitivity is no more than a foundation for learning, so build on your foundation by trying out as many learning-activity ideas in the book as possible.
- As for discipline, read Chapter 3 carefully, especially if you scored low on the Discipline questions (Questions 6–10). Try out any new ideas.

Low self-instruction aptitude

You don't have much confidence in your own language sensitivity or self-discipline.

- For language sensitivity, a lot of this might be due to poor experiences at school – but now that you are an independent learner, you can choose what activities suit **you.** Remember that speaking another language is **natural** (half the world's population can do it), not some magical gift. Try out as many as possible of the activities in this book. With experience, your confidence will grow.
- Discipline is something you can teach yourself. Read Chapter 3 carefully: set yourself a learning programme, and give yourself a reward for each week you follow it!

If you follow our advice, do this questionnaire again in a few months. Your score should be a lot higher.

Self-instruction experience

Experience is another factor that helps learning – it is stronger than aptitude, in fact. As your language-learning experience grows – especially your 'self-instruction experience', so does your toolkit of strategies to cope with the problems you might meet as an independent learner. Also, experience teaches you to persevere, because you know that early difficulties will only be temporary.

Advice for various levels of experience is given in the boxes below. If you are not sure which level fits you best, try the Self-instruction experience questionnaire in Chapter 5 (p38).

Veteran learners

You have good experience and excellent awareness of the factors involved in solo language learning. If you also have a good score on the Self-Instruction Aptitude test and strong motivation to learn (▶ 'Motivation', p12), you have excellent prospects of success in your next foreign language. Even so, read the rest of the book, as there will almost certainly be a good many activities that you have not tried, and which can boost your learning even further.

Fully-fledged learners

You have some teach-yourself experience and a reasonable-to-good awareness of the factors involved in solo language learning. If you also have a good score on the Self-Instruction Aptitude test and good motivation to learn (▶ 'Motivation', p12), you have a good chance of success in your next self-instructed language. By reading through the book carefully, however, and by trying the activities that are new to you, you will greatly boost your chance of success. It is also worth reading through the bullet points in the Novices Box (N) below.

Novice learners

You are relatively new to self-instruction in foreign languages. This book will be invaluable to you: read it carefully, and try out as many ideas as possible. Here are some key points, given to us by experienced learners, which are worth noting:

- Until you have enough words and grammar for basic communication (one year or so with an easy European language, two years or more with a difficult one), learning can sometimes seem pointless. Keep at it: once you get there, learning is much more fun!

- It's easy to run out of steam when you're learning on your own: there's no obligation to do homework or turn up to class, and no classmates to look forward to meeting each week. Instead, try to set up regular working routines, and meet up regularly with other learners or native speakers – see Chapter 3 and Chapter 4 (▶ 'People as a learning resource', p23).

- Understanding native-speaker speech is the most difficult skill to master. Get lots of practice with cassettes and videos (see Chapter 9). When you do meet native speakers, don't panic: understand what you can, and ignore the rest. It'll come in time.

- Language is not just words and grammar, it's a means of communicating with people. So get practice in **using** your language right from the beginning: see Chapter 4 (▶ 'People as a learning resource', p23), and the chapters on Reading, Listening, Writing and Speaking (Chapters 8–11).

3

Preparing to learn

The previous chapter will have given you more insights into who you are as a learner, and how this can affect your learning speed and strategies. Before we look at specific learning techniques, however, it is worth preparing the ground carefully. This is the purpose of this chapter. We start by looking at the crucial issue of motivation (below); we then give advice on how to analyse your learning needs (p14), for what you need to learn not only influences your motivation, but also your choice of learning methods and goals. How far it is practically possible for you to meet your needs depends on two factors: the learning resources available, and how much time you have: these are discussed in the section on 'Resources' (p16). A key way of keeping up motivation is to set yourself realistic learning goals, matching what you need or would like to learn with the learning resources and time actually available to you – this is the topic of 'Setting learning goals' (p18). Finally, in 'Drawing up a learning programme' (p19), we show how to turn learning goals into personalised, ready-to-use learning plans to structure your learning on a day-by-day basis.

Motivation

What is motivation?

Motivation – the drive that makes you try to achieve your goals – is the power-house of language learning. As mentioned earlier, it is the single most important factor in language-learning success: the more motivation you have, the more likely you are not to give up learning, and hence the more likely you are to succeed.

There are different types of motivation: long-term and short-term, for instance. **Long-term motivation** keeps you chasing your ultimate goal – e.g. that of learning enough Spanish to talk with your Spanish friends next summer. This is obviously important, but so is **short-term motivation**: this is what drives you to do an hour's learning today rather than put it off till tomorrow, or to complete the present unit in your coursebook.

Using and boosting motivation

We will discuss goals in detail in a little while. Before this, here are some tips on how to make the best of your existing motivation, and how to enhance it. We have arranged the tips according to the source of motivation; read through the list, and tick the motivation sources which already apply to you. Then, for the sources which you have ticked, try out our advice. For those which you haven't ticked, think about how you might develop these areas into sources of motivation (e.g. Arabic culture: watch films, buy books, etc in order to build up an interest in Arabic art, architecture and literature).

- **Need** to learn the language. Need may be for career, exam, holidays, residence, study, family, romance, etc. Identify your needs by getting a piece of paper and writing down as many ways as possible in which knowing your chosen language will improve your quality of life. Copy out these 'reasons to be multilingual' and stick them in the front of your exercise-book or folder or on the wall above your desk: read them every time you feel that learning the language is hard going. If you use a coursebook, make sure you choose one that fits your needs (▶ 'Choosing and using teach-yourself packages', p20). Try to find practice activities that suit your needs too (for career, try e-mailing foreign colleagues or contacts; for family, write or ring them; and for romance, your imagination's the limit!).

- Whatever your need, **visiting the country** where the language is spoken or making friends with **native speakers** will increase your motivation to learn – so try to visit the country, or get in touch with native speakers in your own country. Working with **other learners** of the same language can also help: pleasure in the contacts you make can motivate you to keep on learning together. See Chapter 4 (▶ 'People as a learning resource', p23) for more advice.

- A liking for the **culture**, history, people and language is another good motivator. Try reading books and watching videos to back up your study. If your command of the foreign language is low, these needn't be in the foreign language: the important thing is to learn to appreciate the culture.

- Many people take pleasure in **language-learning** in general. Regard what you're doing as a hobby, not as a chore!

- It is a big help if language-learning is a **family** business. If you want to catch up with your kids/parents/partner, practise the language with them. If you're the only one learning the language, why not persuade another family member to try the language as well, to keep you company? If you're learning the mother tongue of a parent or partner, persuade him or her to set aside a 'language hour' every day or two when, come what may, you talk in their language rather than English (after tea/supper is often a good time).

- Have **realistic expectations**. For instance that, after working at a new language an hour a day and several days a week for a year or so, you should be able to get by in a rough-and-ready sort of way ('talking with hands and feet', as the Dutch call it) in a foreign country. Don't set your expectations too low: given the right conditions, any adult can learn to survive in a foreign language. Nor too high: if you think you'll be chatting away fluently and understanding every word said to you six months after starting a new language, you'll be disappointed, and might risk giving up as a result.

- **Believe in yourself!** Remember that half the world's population can get by in more than one language, so it can't be that hard!

- Boost your short-term motivation by **making your learning more enjoyable**. If you are a beginner or elementary learner, choose an enjoyable, bright, interesting course package. Learn with people you like (especially native speakers!). Use enjoyable reading and listening materials: comics, magazines, TV games shows, videos, etc.

What if motivation starts flagging?

Every learner goes through times when they don't feel like learning, and some might even occasionally question the value of carrying on with the language. Here are a few tips on how to get through these sticky patches without giving up.

Like learning any new skill, learning a new language can be hard work at first – you stand more chance of succeeding if you accept the fact and buckle down to it. Sometimes you might feel you're putting in a lot of present pain for a very distant gain: in this case, remember language learning also has immediate **benefits**:

- Language learning should be fun in itself most of the time. If it isn't, change your materials or activities: see 'making learning more enjoyable' above.

- Remember: no matter how low your knowledge, you can always get much more out of a visit to the country than a non-speaker!

- Language learning is a good way of meeting people (see 'Using and boosting motivation' above, p12, for tips on how to meet them). Native speakers are often delighted to help someone learn their language, especially if it is one not so widely studied.

- The first stage is the hardest: once you get to a level where you can function in a rough-and-ready way in the language, using it becomes fun and learning it becomes easy.

Self-discipline is also vital! Sometimes you might have to be tough on yourself – especially, try not to break your working routines. On the other hand, there's no point banging your head against a brick wall. If a text is incomprehensible or an activity too difficult, drop it and do something else. The knowledge will come in time, by other means.

Avoid long gaps in learning. After a few weeks of not learning, you risk feeling that you have slid back a long way. If this does happen to you, don't despair. Set up a quick, intensive revision programme: you'll be surprised how quickly you will come back up to par.

Analysing your needs

From the previous section, we know that 'need to learn' is an important source of language-learning motivation. It also determines the crucial question of what and how you should be learning. This section describes how to analyse your needs so that you can customise your own learning programme – thus enabling you to learn what **you** need, which will boost your motivation further.

The technique – **'needs analysis'** – involves matching the situations in which you need to use the language with the language skills and areas that correspond to those situations. Imagine, for example, that you are travelling to Germany as a member of an amateur orchestra in which the working language is German. Perhaps all travel and accommodation arrangements are already made for you, but you will need to be able to understand the conductor's directions at rehearsals. Therefore listening skills and musical terminology will be **essential** to you – but not practical transactions at a travel agent's, say. If, on the other hand, you are going on a backpacking holiday in Bolivia, it will be essential that you are able to arrange your own transport in the local language. You may also require additional listening practice in order to cope with the local accent.

You should write down your needs analysis – as in the two examples below, written by someone going to study engineering at a French university. This will enable you to work out your needs in greater detail, and will give a basic action plan which you can refer to later:

1 Start by taking a few sheets of paper. Turn them horizontally (landscape format) and divide them into two columns (the left-hand one should be narrower).

2 Think of the **most typical situations** in which you will be needing or wanting to use the language. Put one situation in the left-hand column of each page.

3 In the right hand column, describe **what skills are involved in each situation**. Make notes for each of the following areas: Reading, Writing, Listening, Speaking, Grammar, Vocabulary, and Target country knowledge.

Situation	Language skills involved
1. Attending engineering lectures in my year abroad	■ Good <u>listening</u> comprehension at normal speed (essential). ■ <u>Writing</u>: note-taking from lectures. Examination papers (!) ■ <u>Reading</u>: finding and using background reading before the lectures (I've been told it could help). ■ <u>Vocabulary</u>: core technical vocabulary, especially maths! ■ <u>Speaking</u>: none (apparently classes there are very formal). ■ <u>Grammar</u>: not relevant here. ■ <u>Target country knowledge</u>: finding out more about the syllabus, teaching methods and assessment in the foreign university might help.

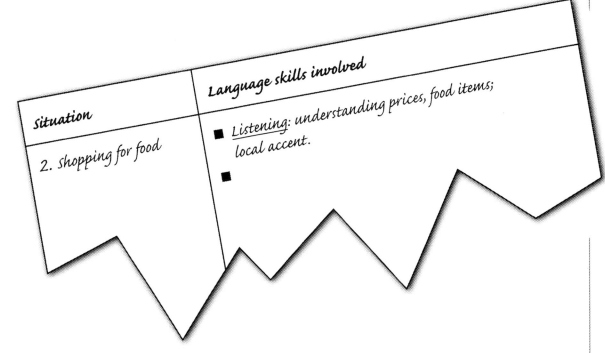

Situation	Language skills involved
2. shopping for food	■ <u>Listening</u>: understanding prices, food items; local accent. ■

Resources

The list of needs which you have drawn up is the raw material for setting your learning goals. But for goals to be realistic, you have to consider the resources at your disposal. The main resources are learning means – course materials, classes, etc – and time.

Learning means

What learning means are available?

Independent learning needn't just mean sitting in your room with a book and a cassette player. Below we list some possible learning resources – which of these is available to you?

- suitable and affordable classes?
- suitable and affordable self-instruction packages?
- a self-access centre in a school, college or university?
- foreign-language settings: the foreign-language country, of course, but also foreign restaurants, social groups, etc in the UK?
- native speakers?
- other learners?
- authentic listening and reading materials (including newspapers and magazines, satellite TV, the Internet, etc)?

How can I get hold of them?

The easiest way to join classes is to ring up your local adult education centre, college or university and ask if classes are available. As for self-instruction materials, first try browsing in bookshops and the biggest public library in your area. Here are some more tips:

- Try to visit your local college or university language centre or self-access centre, and compare course packages. If possible, join it – if you aren't a student, ring local colleges and universities and ask if members of the public can pay to use the facilities. Even if this isn't possible, ask if you can phone a language advisor: most will be glad to give advice on a one-off basis.

- Contact teachers (e.g. via your local adult education centre), or people who work in a language centre or language department, and ask which courses they would recommend.

- Get friends in the foreign country to send you reading materials, cassettes, etc.

- Contact the foreign country's tourist board or embassy: they may have materials in the language.

For details on how to get in touch with native speakers, other learners, etc, see ▶ 'People as a learning resource' (p23). For details on how to select the best course package for you, see ▶ 'Choosing and using teach-yourself packages' (p20).

Which resources should I use?

The answer to this question depends firstly on your **needs**: thus the engineering student about to study abroad (in our example above) might use cassettes to improve her lecture listening, but talk to French native-speaker students in the UK to build up her knowledge about the French university system.

KEY TERMS

Authentic materials = materials produced for native speakers, not for language learners – e.g. off-air videos, newspapers, comics, etc.

Secondly, as we mentioned in the Introduction, the choice of learning resources also depends on your **proficiency** in the foreign language. If you're a **beginner**, you might be better finding a class, at least for the first year or two – unless you just want a quick-and-dirty smattering of the language, in which case a teach-yourself course avoids the commitment of having to attend classes. Even if you do take a class, it's a good idea to use self-instruction as a back-up – e.g. to fill in gaps or to give more learning time. But if you aren't able to attend a class, this is what you can do:

- Firstly, buy a package (if you can afford it, buy two!). See ▶ 'Choosing and using teach-yourself packages' (p20) for tips on choosing and using packages.

- Use your local self-access centre regularly, trying out various learning packages; try using easy authentic listening or reading materials as a variation.

- Try to find somebody who is also learning the language (you don't have to be exactly at the same level). This will help keep you motivated and provide a partner for speaking practice.

- Whether or not you attend a class, buy a decent bilingual dictionary (▶ 'Choosing and using dictionaries', p25, for tips on dictionary-buying).

If you are at **intermediate or advanced** proficiency, it is a good idea to get used to using authentic materials in the foreign language: the Reading and Listening chapters (8 and 9) will give you useful advice here. But also:

- If you can, get a textbook or join a class suitable for your proficiency level, to give a 'serious' base to your learning.

- Buy a good bilingual dictionary (as big as you can afford).

- Get hold of a grammar reference book (as part of a coursebook, or stand-alone).

- Use your local self-access centre: watch videos, listen to the radio or cassettes, watch satellite TV, read easy books and magazines.

- If you have access to the Internet, start searching for sites in the foreign country (▶ **[R16]** *Surfing the Net*) or join chat-rooms in the foreign language.

- Try to find native speakers to talk to: learning will be such fun that you won't think of giving up!

Another key principle in selecting learning means is '**the more the merrier**'. Here are some possible combinations of learning means to choose:

- Use a teach-yourself package and go to a class.

- Use two published packages, not just one (different coursebooks tend to focus on different aspects of the language).

- Vary your learning activities – e.g. watch videos and talk to native speakers.

- When in the foreign country, don't abandon your study programme (a combination of language study and real-life 'immersion' is the most powerful learning combination).

How should I use these resources?

General advice on using learning resources – especially teach-yourself packages, other people, and dictionaries – is given in Chapter 4.

Time resources

The amount of time available is a crucial factor in setting yourself realistic language-learning goals. Ask yourself the following questions:

- How much time can I afford to spend each week? (Be realistic here, not idealistic!) – e.g. six hours.

- Over how many sessions a week can I spread that time? (Remember: a little every day is better than a lot once a week) – e.g. an hour a day, Monday to Friday, plus an hour at the weekend.

- Is there a clear deadline that I have to meet? – e.g. leave for the foreign country or take an examination on a certain date.

The key to using your time resources well is to set aside a regular time-slot for learning. Ideal is 'dead time' not useful for anything else: in the bus or train to work, while doing housework or walking the dog, etc.

Other resources

You should also consider other resources related to your learning environment:

- Where can you study? At home? On the bus?

- Is your concentration likely to be disrupted by telephone calls, children, etc? (Try to find a quiet time or place)

- What technical equipment do you have access to? Walkman (essential for listening practice)? Video player (book a daily slot, or the rest of your household will get in before you)? Computer (there are some nice language-learning CD-ROMs about, but you may have to wait to use them till the kids have gone to bed)?

Setting learning goals

Setting effective goals – i.e. deciding what standard you want to get to, in which skills and/or language areas, and in how much time – is a key success factor. Effective goals are relevant, realistic, specific, timed and measurable: let us look in detail at what this means. 'Analysing your needs' (p14) explained how to carry out an effective needs analysis: this should ensure that your goals are **relevant** to your needs. But they must also be **realistic** in time, as we pointed out in 'Time resources' (above): you may be in desperate need to gain a high level of fluency in your spoken language, yet if you are only a beginner with just a month ahead of you before travelling abroad, you will have to narrow down your immediate goals to just a few survival skills in typical situations.

It is also important to be as **specific** as possible: specify how many textbook pages you want to cover, say, or how many words you want to learn. With vaguely formulated goals, it can be hard to know when you have achieved them, and this can be demotivating after a while. So don't just say 'I want to improve my grammar' – say 'I want to learn all regular verb forms of the indicative by the end of this month'.

This example also shows the importance of **setting a time limit** for each goal ('by such-and-such time I must be able to do such-and-such a thing'): this will also help you ensure that your goal is specific enough. And don't just think in terms of **long-term** goals, e.g. 'to be able to talk about my studies to a native speaker in six months' time'. Also think of **short-term** goals, e.g. 'to get through a coursebook unit each week' or 'to be able to write a paragraph about "my family" by Saturday'.

Finally, state in what way you intend to **measure** whether you have achieved your goals (this will also help you check whether your goals are realistic and specific). For instance, if you say 'I want to talk about topic X at a rate of 150 words per minute instead of my present rate of 100', you can measure whether you have met this goal by using a tape recorder. Finding ways to measure achievement is not always an easy thing to do, however. This is why every learning technique presented in this book includes a section on 'How to assess results'. Once you have tried out some of the techniques and measured your performance in the ways we suggest, it will become easier for you to set and measure your own targets independently.

Finally, when you set yourself a learning goal, also set yourself a **reward** for when you achieve it (rent a video, go to the pub, buy yourself something nice ...). Do this for daily tasks as well as for weekly goals – e.g. 'I'll (only) give myself a beer or a chocolate when I've done half-an-hour's learning'.

Drawing up a learning programme

Armed with all the information from this chapter, you should now spend half an hour drawing up a learning programme (see example on the next page). Making it won't take up much learning time in the long run, as one learning programme should keep you going for several weeks. Here's how:

1   At the top of the page, write down your long-term goals.

2   Underneath, write your weekly goals.

3   Divide the rest of the page into two columns.

4   On the left, for each day of the week, jot down one or two time-and-place slots when you could find 20–30 minutes for language learning.

5   Opposite each slot, write down what you could do in it; try to vary your activities.

6   At the bottom of the page, write down your week's reward.

7   Copy it out and tape it into the front of your coursebook or your language notebook/file.

8   Use Tippex to make any minor changes from week to week (e.g. a different reward).

Learning programme

Long-term goal: by the summer, to talk simple Dutch with my girlfriend's family, and to understand the gist of what they are saying to me.

Goal Week 1: do Unit 1 (Teach Yourself Dutch), and learn how to pronounce 'Hoegaarden'.

Goal Week 2: do Unit 2.

Goal Week 3: do Unit 3, and talk for 3 minutes with Hanneke without switching to English!

Timetable

MONDAY MORNING: *on bus to college*	*Read coursebook.*
TUESDAY MORNING: *on bus to college*	*Listen to cassette dialogues.*
WEDNESDAY 2–3 *(free period): college open learning centre*	*Do language lab exercises.*
THURSDAY EVENING: *Hanneke's place*	*Do dialogues and speaking exercises together.*
FRIDAY 2–3: *(free period): open learning centre*	*Do some writing with a dictionary.*

Reward: treat myself to a pint of Hoegaarden at the Bierrex on Friday night!

---

chapter

4

Getting started

Now that you have set yourself a learning programme, you are ready to learn. This chapter gives information and advice on four key resources in self-instructed language learning: published teach-yourself packages, other people, dictionaries, and grammar books. It also gives some techniques to improve your general learning effectiveness, such as the crucial question of how to remember the words and grammar which you meet, and what to do if you already know a similar language to the one which you are working on.

Choosing and using teach-yourself packages

If you have decided to use a published teach-yourself package to help you learn, here are some tips on what to do next.

Look before you leap

The most important piece of advice is to choose your package carefully. Visit several bookshops to browse through what packages are available; take the 'Tips for choosing a teach-yourself package' (p21) with you to vet the packages you find. Also, go to a couple of local libraries, borrow a selection of courses if possible, check them against the tips, and try working through a unit of each.

Be careful with **mail-order** courses, as you can't browse before buying. Most are more expensive than courses on bookshop shelves, and they may not be as enjoyable or up to date (the September 1990 *Which? Report*, though it's a bit dated, is still useful reading here). And don't believe adverts proclaiming some miracle method that will make language learning easier than conventional (and cheaper) courses: quite simply, there is no magic short-cut to learning a foreign language, and you will be better off in the long run with a decent, all-round course that makes learning enjoyable. We recommend you only buy a mail-order course after you've found a package in the same series (it needn't be the right language, as long as you can get an idea of the publisher's house style) at a public library, FE college or university, and checked it against the 'Tips for choosing a teach-yourself package' on the next page.

TIPS for choosing a teach-yourself package

1 Read the information on the front and back covers, and flick through the book – does the package **fit your learning goals** (see Chapter 3)? Check especially:

- Proficiency level (e.g. beginner, elementary)
- Skills and language areas (e.g. conversation, grammar)
- Subject field (e.g. holidays, business, general)
- Thoroughness (e.g. a quick introduction, or a thorough grounding in the language)

2 Does it come with **audio cassettes**? Cassettes are a must, because listening is a crucial skill for most learners – so they are well worth the extra cost!

3 Is it **up to date**? Check the year of publication of the present edition – ignore the impression year, which just tells you when this batch was (re)printed. This is usually on the reverse of the coursebook title page.

4 Give the coursebook a **physical check-up:**

- Does the binding seem solid? (Each page is going to be turned many times!)
- If you're taking it on holiday, will it fit in a jacket pocket or handbag?
- Is the foreign-language print-size big enough to read easily?

5 Look inside the book, at the information before and after the actual learning units. A good coursebook has:

- A **chapter list** giving the main points (grammar, vocabulary, etc) covered – not just snappy unit titles! An **index** is even better.
- **Two full alphabetical vocabulary lists,** one English > foreign language, and one foreign language > English (beware: many courses only give the latter!).
- **Grammar and pronunciation reference** sections.
- **Exercise answers.** This is particularly important when you don't have a teacher.

6 Now look at a typical unit – i.e. somewhere near the middle of the book. There should be:

- **Foreign-language texts** giving realistic examples of the sort of language that you need (e.g. restaurant dialogues, business letters, etc). These shouldn't be too long (1 page maximum).
- **Vocabulary lists,** preferably with the English equivalents in parallel columns (to make memorising easier), and preferably not too long (twenty words at a time is plenty).
- Clear, reader-friendly **grammar explanations,** with tables where necessary (these may be at the back of the book).
- Plenty of **practice exercises** that look varied and enjoyable. This is crucial! As a rule of thumb, for every page of dialogue or grammar information there should be at least a page of practice exercises. Check that they cover the right **balance of skills** for your goals (e.g. a holiday course should have plenty of speaking and listening, with some reading of signs, menus, etc, but little writing).

Counting the cost

The cost of course packages is a key issue for many people. Here are some tips:

• **Borrow** rather than buy. Public libraries generally have reasonably up-to-date packages for the more common foreign languages. Or try to join a self-access centre at a local college or university. (See 'Learning means, p16, for more details on getting hold of materials.)

• If buying **second-hand**, from newspaper adverts or second-hand bookshops, carefully check the publication year (Tip 3 in 'Tips for choosing a teach-yourself package' above). Anything over ten years old risks containing old-fashioned language.

Changing courses

Even if you choose carefully, you may find that a teach-yourself package isn't working for you. The important thing is not to blame yourself for being a 'bad language learner'. Try out another package. Try also using some of the ideas in this book to add variety to your learning. Of course, you might quite simply be the sort of person who learns better in a class, at least until you've got a decent grounding in the language – in this case, it would be worth making extra efforts to find out about what classes are available in your area.

Using a published teach-yourself package

Most of the techniques in this book apply just as well to learning from packages as to learning completely independently. Here, however, are a few extra tips on how to get the best out of your teach-yourself package.

Planning

Even if most of your learning is guided by the package, make sure you set **learning goals** and draw up a **learning programme**: see Chapter 3 (p18) for details.

Vary course package work with your **own choice of materials** (e.g. videos, magazines), speaking to native speakers and other learners, etc.

Foreign-language texts

When you come to a new text or dialogue in your coursebook, don't use the **vocabulary list** the first time you read or listen – only use it the second time. This will give you practice in trying to work out the meaning of what you hear or read when you are in the native country.

If you need to note down **English translations of key words**, do this on a separate sheet rather than between the lines or in the margin of the text or dialogue. Otherwise, each time you read, your eyes will skip the foreign words and read the English instead.

Language explanations

If you find the language explanations in the coursebook hard to understand, ask someone who knows the language well to explain it (a non-native speaker may well be better than a native speaker here, because the non-native speaker was once in your position!). Or check in another coursebook: its explanations might be clearer. Also, regularly re-read grammar explanations from earlier in the coursebook: the more experience you have of the language, the more sense they will make.

Practice activities

If your coursebook has a lot of **mechanical grammar exercises** (e.g. changing present verbs into the past), these can get rather boring. Don't feel you've got to do them all: see Chapter 7 for ideas for more enjoyable grammar activities.

With old-fashioned coursebooks, there may be very **few practice activities** apart from grammar exercises. In such a case, use your needs analysis to set up a practice programme that suits your learning goals (see Chapter 3, p18, for step-by-step instructions), then choose your activities from the DIY techniques in Part 2 (Chapters 6–11).

Cassette work

Get yourself a **walkman** – then you can do cassette work anywhere.

Some learners use cassettes in the **car**. For road-safety reasons, *DON'T DO PAUSE, REWIND AND REPEAT WORK WHILE YOU'RE DRIVING*: operating the cassette player and the high attention needed for drill-type exercises could both be fatally distracting. We recommend only doing 'extensive' listening in the car, i.e. listening to long texts, such as songs, to get the general gist or for entertainment, without stopping and rewinding.

Speaking to cassettes can feel **embarrassing** if others can hear you. Try whispering (as long as you are producing some sound, you are learning). Or schedule your speaking practice for times and places where you are alone.

Ready reference

Your coursebook isn't only a learning tool. Use it as a vocabulary and grammar reference handbook as well: take it with you when you are travelling in the native country, or use it to help you write letters in the foreign language.

People as a learning resource

Learning a language independently, whether you are working from a package or from your own choice of materials, doesn't necessarily mean learning on your own. Help from other people can be extremely valuable, as we explain in this section.

Who can help?

Here we list five types of people who can help you: native speakers, fellow learners, competent non-native speakers, teachers, and language advisors.

Native speakers

If you can get in touch with native speakers, don't waste the opportunity! They can provide you with:

- a chance to actually use the language: even the slightest achievement in communication will boost your motivation;
- information about the foreign language (but bear in mind that not all native speakers are fully aware of how their own language works);
- first-hand factual information about the foreign culture;
- feedback on your spoken and written output.

A good way of using native speakers is to set up a **tandem learning** partnership. This involves teaming up with a native speaker of your foreign language who is willing to learn your own native language (▶ **[W10]** *Letters and e-mail* on how to find a partner). You spend half the time on the language you are learning, and half the time on the language your partner is learning, which allows you to ask for help more freely than if your partner was just doing you a favour. Many of the techniques described in this book mention tandem learning (though you could also use them with a native speaker who is not a tandem partner).

Fellow learners

If it proves difficult to get in touch with native speakers, or if you still find it intimidating, why not try a few sessions with a learning partner, or '**study buddy**', i.e. somebody who is in the same position as you? It doesn't matter if your levels are not identical: the most confident of the two will teach the other and you will both learn in the process. A study buddy can help you in many ways – for instance, by:

- keeping up your discipline (it's more difficult to call off a session if somebody else is also involved);

- acting as a partner in speaking tasks (don't worry about picking up each other's mistakes – practice is more important than accuracy for the moment);

- helping you figure out things that you might not understand if you were by yourself;

- supporting you through the learning process.

Competent non-native speakers

You may know somebody who has a good command of the language without necessarily being a native speaker. These people can be very helpful because they are likely to understand your problems. They too were once in your position and probably had to figure out solutions that they can now share with you.

Acting as a competent speaker yourself (by helping another learner who is at an earlier stage than you) can also be a useful experience, as it will help you revise and clarify what you already know. You may also discover some gaps in your knowledge, and this will draw your attention to problems that you still need to address.

Teachers

Obviously, if you know a teacher of your foreign language, he or she will be an ideal source of information and feedback about the language itself. If you are attending a class, do not hesitate to consult your teacher about areas that you have been covering independently, even if they are not related to the syllabus. It's a teacher's job to help you learn!

Language advisors

Some language centres have duty advisors whose job is to help people make the most of the resources available. If there is one in your language centre, make sure that you arrange an appointment to discuss your needs and goals.

A language advisor is not a teacher, and will not normally explain grammar points, correct your mistakes and so on. Instead, the advisor will help you analyse your needs, set realistic goals, find out what resources are available, and get organised. You may also use the language advisor to help you monitor your progress at regular intervals and keep you on track.

How to contact them

Native speakers

You can get in touch with native speakers during visits abroad, by joining conversation classes, by advertising 'conversation exchanges' on a language-centre notice-board, by going to restaurants, or by joining an expatriate church or social club. If you know people abroad, write to them in their language; ask them to send you reading and listening materials (magazines, songs, cassette letters, etc), or to write about their daily life. You could also join a discussion group that uses the foreign language on the Internet (▶ **[R16]** *Surfing the Net*).

Fellow-learners and other non-native speakers

Here, try advertising in local libraries, language centres, etc. Get in touch with old classmates (if appropriate). Many people make language-learning into a whole-family project! Arrange to meet regularly, to discuss and correct each other's work, or just to chat in the foreign language. Also, teaching the language you are learning to another family member or a flatmate is an excellent revision and practice method.

Language advisors and teachers

Find out whether your local resource centre has a language advising service. If not, perhaps you can join a class to complement your personal learning programme.

Choosing and using dictionaries

After course packages and people, a third crucial learning tool is the dictionary.

Choosing a dictionary

As with any tool, you need to use the right dictionary for the job in hand. The two main types are **bilingual dictionaries** (those which list words and their translations) and **monolingual dictionaries** (those which list words and their definitions in the same language). We describe these and other types of dictionary below.

Pocket bilingual dictionaries

As long as they are 'two-way' (i.e. English > foreign language and foreign language > English), bilingual dictionaries can be used for both decoding (i.e. for reading and listening) and encoding (i.e. for writing and speaking). If you are only beginning to learn a language, a two-way pocket bilingual dictionary will probably give you all the information that you need at this stage. It is also the obvious choice if you are travelling abroad for a short holiday or if you can't carry a larger volume for some other reason.

- Go for one that gives a phonetic transcript of the words, so that you know how to pronounce new words. Those which use the International Phonetic Alphabet (IPA) are best, because it is the most accurate system, and the same symbol will represent the same one sound in any language of the world. The IPA symbols used for one particular language can be learnt surprisingly quickly.

KEY TERMS

Decoding = recognition = finding out what foreign-language words mean while reading or listening.

Encoding = production = finding the foreign-language words that you need to form your own messages while writing or speaking.

- Compare entries for the same three or four words in different dictionaries before you buy. A slightly larger book will not necessarily contain more (or better presented) information!

- Not many pocket dictionaries have space for examples of how words are used in context, but this is certainly a plus if it is available.

- Some dictionaries contain basic grammar summaries and verb tables, and this can be an advantage if you are not planning to be carrying many books at once.

Larger bilingual dictionaries

If you continue studying beyond survival level, you will soon find that you need more information than pocket dictionaries can provide. Obviously, a large volume can contain more information, but again look carefully:

- Try to consult people who make regular use of both languages (advanced learners, language teachers, bilingual students, etc) for advice.

- Check the number of words it contains (this will be stated on the cover or in the Introduction). You need at least 70,000 words each way.

- Look up a few words (from English to the foreign language and vice versa), including a technical word, a colloquial expression, and a word that has lots of different meanings (such as 'go', 'as', etc in English).

- Make sure the dictionary offers short examples for the main possible uses of a word.

Monolingual dictionaries

Monolingual dictionaries are generally used for decoding, i.e. for listening and reading – though they can also give a useful second opinion on a word you may find in an English > foreign-language dictionary. They tend to be most useful once you are able to deal with relatively extended texts (listening and/or reading) in the foreign language. By defining words in the foreign language, they provide you with:

- a level of nuance that no bilingual dictionary could offer;

- the opportunity to drop translation completely and start thinking directly in the foreign language;

- other words that are used in the definition and have a similar meaning;

- examples of the word in use.

Pictorial dictionaries

If you don't even know the name of certain objects in your own language (like different types of wild flowers, the parts of a car engine, etc), you may find pictorial dictionaries useful. Each page shows a series of pictures related to a particular topic. Small number tags on each item refer you to the name of that item in both languages: hence they can be used both for decoding and for encoding.

Specialist dictionaries

Your work may require you to use specialist terms – e.g. business or scientific vocabulary – that are not found in general dictionaries. Being a user of English, you are in a privileged position because there is a huge variety of bilingual (or even multilingual) dictionaries available in a wide range of subjects.

On-line and CD-ROM dictionaries

If you normally use a word processor to write in the foreign language, on-line and CD-ROM dictionaries are useful, comprehensive and fast tools. You simply type in a word, and its translation and/or definition is displayed instantly.

Tourist phrasebooks

Some people find these useful as a back-up to a regular dictionary, but they're no good for learning a language by themselves (you need a decent coursebook as well).

Using a dictionary

How often should I look up words?

This depends on the task you are performing. If you are just reading a newspaper, a novel or a magazine, you will probably be focusing on gist rather than detail, and should not worry too much about understanding every single word (▶ **[R5]** *Extensive reading*). In this case, you can restrict dictionary use to a few essential key words.

If, on the other hand, you are reading a text to improve your vocabulary and grammar, you may wish to look up every word that you don't know (▶ **[R6]** *Intensive reading*). However, this can become frustratingly slow. Restrict yourself to twenty minutes or so of this technique at a time, or allow yourself a set number of words to look up (the first twenty words that you don't know, for example). Then put the dictionary aside and continue reading without it.

Obviously, if you are doing **translation work**, you will need to look up every word of which you are even slightly unsure.

Decoding (reading and listening)

You can either use a bilingual or a monolingual dictionary here. Although it might seem relatively easy to look up a foreign-language word, it is not entirely problem-free:

- In languages that use a different script, searches take longer than normal. This soon gets easier with practice, however (▶ **[R3]** *Learning a new script*).

- The form of the word that is shown in the dictionary may differ from the form of the word in the text in which you found it (e.g. unless your dictionary includes suitable cross-references, you will never find the word *'went'* unless you already know that it is one of the forms of the verb *'go'*).

- If you are looking up a word that you have heard, but not seen in writing, your guess about its spelling might be wrong. Try alternative spellings. It could also be that you have misinterpreted where one word ends and the next one begins.

- Words that are colloquial, technical, or specific to one particular region may not be included in the dictionary that you are using. Try reading more of the text to find other clues.

Encoding (writing and speaking)

Only a bilingual or pictorial dictionary can help here. The effects of poor dictionary use, however, can range from slightly odd to incomprehensible or even hilarious. An awareness of the basic pitfalls should help:

KEY TERMS

Source language = in dictionary work or translating, the language you are working out of.

Target language = in dictionary work or translating, the language you are working into.

- Be aware what word category you are looking for. The verb *'to walk'* and the noun *'a walk'* will come in different parts of the entry for *'walk'* in an English–foreign-language dictionary, and may well have totally different foreign-language equivalents (in French, for example, *'marcher'* and *'une balade'* respectively).

- If you are translating words that are part of a phrase, bear in mind that the target language may express the same idea in a completely different way from the source language: *'to run out'* is unlikely to translate as *'to run'* + *'out'* in the foreign language.

- One source-language word may correspond to two very different target-language words. For instance, when translating the English word *'bottom'* in *'I want to get to the bottom of this'*, you will have to choose your foreign-language equivalent carefully!

- Alternatively, the precise sense or nuance which you want may simply not be given in the target language.

Fortunately, a few precautions can be taken:

- Don't automatically pick the first equivalent that you come across in a dictionary. Quickly look through all the 'sub-entries' devoted to your source-language word (e.g. the English word *bar*): first check out all the different grammatical forms (*bar (n.)*, *bar (v.)*, etc) to find the form you need; then check out the different meaning categories (*bar = rod, bar = pub, bar = prohibition*) to find the meaning you need. Finally, read carefully through the whole sub-entry for the right meaning category, and choose the best equivalent. This may be on the basis of an example phrase, but if no examples are given, you may have to use the …

- … Back-translation technique. When working into the foreign language, to check that you have chosen the correct word if several foreign-language options are given, look up each option in the foreign-language > English half of the dictionary until the English equivalent matches the sense which you wanted.

- If the target language word would normally undergo changes depending on grammatical rules (verb agreement, gender, case, etc), make sure you use it in the correct form, which may be different from the one given in the dictionary.

- Choose a dictionary that gives examples of the words in context whenever you can.

The dictionary as a learning aid

Dictionaries be used to help you learn as well as for understanding or producing messages. Here are some tips.

- After you have looked up words or phrases while reading or writing, write the most useful ones out again in your language notebook (▶ 'Language notebooks', p30) and memorise them.

- Note down the pronunciation as well (if that's not obvious from the spelling).

- When you look up a foreign word, look at the words around it that seem to be related (e.g. German *Haus, Hausfrau, häuslich* …), and note down any that seem especially useful. Learn them as a family. In such a case, it is probably better to settle for recognition command (listening or reading) rather than production command (speaking or writing) – for the latter, you will also need practice in meeting and using the words in real sentences.

Choosing a grammar book

Getting a grammar reference source that is right for you can make your learning much easier, and enable you to work better on improving your accuracy.

Tips for beginners

As a beginner, you can probably find all the grammar you need in a good coursebook. Check the grammar sections using the rest of this checklist. If some aspects fail to meet the criteria, look for another coursebook that can fill the gap. If you go for a dedicated grammar book, make sure that it meets the criteria for your level.

Are you looking for something that guides you step by step through the basic structure of the language in a logical progression?

If you are a beginner, or if you are planning a thorough revision of the grammar, it is a good idea to look for a structured, 'progressive' grammar book (i.e. one that starts with the basics and gradually tackles more complex rules). Don't just look at stand-alone grammar books: you may find the grammar sections of general course books easier to follow.

Do you need a book where you can check specific grammar points whenever you have a problem?

If this is the case (or if your level is more advanced), a reference book may be just what you need in order to provide a deeper insight into specific topics. When you choose your reference book, check how easy it is to find the answer to a particular question (e.g. do you need to be familiar with complex terminology in order to know where to look?).

Depth and breadth

At the initial levels, all you want is a general overview of basic structures, without going into all the exceptions to the rules. At more advanced levels, you need greater detail because you will be coming across more sophisticated language and expressing more complex ideas yourself.

Should the explanations be in English?

Normally it is easier to understand the explanations if they are in your mother tongue. Books that explain the rules in English may even compare the two languages to warn you against the differences and make use of the similarities. At more advanced levels, however, you may wish to do all your thinking in the foreign language.

Grammars written in the foreign language are less likely to be written with speakers of your mother tongue in mind. On the other hand, they often have more depth and they use the same terminology that is used in the foreign country. This is particularly important if you are planning to attend a language course in the foreign country.

Examples

Every grammar book has examples to show how the different rules work. Are there enough examples in the book that you are considering?

Do the examples use a similar vocabulary range to your own? (i.e. can you understand most of them without a dictionary?). If the answer is no, this book is probably not for you.

Does the book have exercises to practice the rules?

Explanations alone may help you understand how the language works (some books are very good at this), but you will only become able to use the rules yourself if you practise them. If your book does not have exercises, it is important that you supplement it with exercises from another source.

Do the exercises use a similar vocabulary range to your own? (i.e. can you tackle most of them without a dictionary?). If the answer is no, this book is probably not for you.

Are the exercises based on single sentences, or are you encouraged to apply the rules within a wider context? If most of the material is sentence-based, you will need to supplement your work with other types of exercises in which the rules are used in context (▶ **[W2]** *Back translation,* **[G6]** *Chop and jumble,* **[W3]** *Creating a gapped text*).

Is there an answer key for the exercises?

This is particularly important if you are working by yourself. If there is no key, you may have to seek other sources of feedback (▶ **[G9]** *Seeking feedback*).

General learning techniques

We turn now from learning resources to general advice on learning efficiently and effectively. We examine five topics: language notebooks, memorising new language, looking back at previous work, getting feedback, and using other languages that you know.

Language notebooks

Take a pocket-sized notebook everywhere you go. Write down any useful words or phrases (just the useful ones: not all!) which you come across in reading or listening, or which you find in a dictionary. In the bus, train or on walks, memorise the items (tip: a clear plastic pocket protects it from the rain!). This technique is especially useful when you are in the foreign country.

Memorisation techniques

Most learners say that memorising words, phrases and grammar is crucial if you want to keep up a steady sense of progress. Here are some tips:

- If you have got rough notes (e.g. in your notebook, or in a margin of your coursebook), write them out 'in neat' in a separate section of your language notebook or a loose-leaf file. The neat information isn't only easier to memorise: the act of writing it out also helps you to remember. Try making your own **grammar tables**, using coloured pens to mark important points. And make a personal **loose-leaf dictionary** (▶ **[V4]** *Word lists*).

- Write down **phrases** (especially from texts and dialogues on which you have worked) rather than individual words, because they stick in the mind better in the long run. But make sure each phrase only has one new word or grammar item: the rest should be items that you already know, to avoid an over-heavy learning load.

- One memorisation technique (especially suitable for studial learners) is the **cover-over** technique. With vocabulary lists or translated dialogues, cover one language with a piece of paper and use the other language as a prompt; when you have tried to guess each hidden word or sentence, uncover it, check if you were right, and repeat the correct version. With vocabulary lists, put a / next to the item the first time you guess it correctly, add a \ to make it into an **X** the second time; in later learning sessions, skip the items marked **X**.

- With **grammar tables**, use the cover-over technique to work your way item by item down or across the table, trying to remember what form comes next. If your **textbook dialogue** isn't translated, work your way down the dialogue line by line, saying what you think comes next.

- Another technique (especially suitable for experiential learners) is simply to **repeat** cassette dialogues, off-air audio and video recordings, etc again and again, until you know them nearly by heart. Or **read out** coursebook dialogues and texts.

- But in both cases, make sure you **write** or **speak out loud** (if you're in a crowded place, whisper or mumble): we remember better when we produce than when we just recognise.

- If a word won't stick, see if you can make a **'keyword-image'**. This is a silly image which puns what the word sounds like in English (the 'keyword') with what it actually means. For example, with the German *Rathaus* (which means town hall), think of rats running out of Hamelin town hall after the Pied Piper. Then you'll never forget it!

- If you're using word-lists or translated dialogues, don't just go from English to the foreign language. Go **the other way** as well.

- Set yourself weekly **memorisation targets** – a certain number of words, or of texts.

- But don't get obsessed by memorisation. **A little often** is best: after about twenty minutes' memorisation work, your brain simply stops remembering. And don't think you have to memorise *every* day: vary your activities: reading, memorising, listening, repeating, speaking, writing …

Revisiting and revising

Learning isn't a one-off business: basically, the more often we do something, the better it sticks in our mind. A key technique is **'revisiting'**: doing activities not just once, but repeating them the next day and even the day after that, until you can do them with ease.

Regular long-term **revision** is also vital: once a month or so, go back and review what you have been doing in the last few weeks. When you revise, you will find that you have 'forgotten' a lot of what you learnt. Don't worry – this is why you're revising! You will find you will learn the items much more quickly the second time, and they will stay in memory much longer. Revision needn't be a formal business: try listening to cassettes and reading texts you have tackled in the past.

Getting feedback

Getting feedback on how well you are learning is important in helping you improve, and giving you a sense of progress: this is why we have included a section on 'How to assess your progress' in all the DIY techniques described in Part 2. Here are some general ways of getting feedback and a sense of progress:

- **Ask other people** (▶ 'People as a learning resource', p23) to give you feedback on speaking or to correct your writing.

- **Count how many pages** of a coursebook or a reading book you can get through in a week. Or **set yourself a target** (e.g. learn five verbs, or read two stories) and a time to reach it in (e.g. by the end of the week). If you can reach the target comfortably, see if you can beat your target time (six days? five days?) the next week (▶ 'Setting learning goals', p18, and 'Drawing up a learning programme', p19).

- After an encounter in the foreign country (e.g. buying something in a shop), **ask yourself how well you performed**. Try giving yourself points out of ten – five for getting the message across, and five for quality of language.

- Register for an **exam,** such as GCSE or Institute of Linguists, in the language.

- For **pronunciation,** record yourself repeating after a cassette in the language lab (or read a coursebook dialogue into a cassette), then check yourself against the original.

- For **writing, vocabulary, grammar:** write (or translate) a short text without a dictionary. Then check the vocabulary with a dictionary, and/or check the grammar with a coursebook.

- See also the techniques described in Part 2: ▶ **[G9]** *Seeking feedback,* **[W16]** *Marking your written performance,* **[S14]** *Marking your spoken performance.*

Using related languages

If you already know something of a language in the same family as the language you are learning, you can use this knowledge to help you – but it can also 'interfere' with the new language. Here are some tips on how to use the 'old' language to help with the new one, and on how to cope with the interference problem.

Using language transfer as a strategy

Make the most of language transfer by looking for common points between the two languages. For example, when you meet a new word (e.g. *pensar > to think,* in Spanish) look for words which are roughly similar in form and meaning in a related language (e.g. *penser* in French): the link will make the new word easy to remember. If you see a new word in a text, try to guess it by asking yourself whether it resembles a word in a related language whose meaning would fit in the context. A couple of extra tips are worth mentioning:

- The links may sometimes be disguised by sound changes – for example, the sound *p* in English (and other Germanic languages, like Dutch or Danish) has changed to *pf* or *f* in equivalent German words (pipe > *Pfeife;* grip > *Griff*). These systematic sound changes are worth looking out for and learning.

- Look for similarities between grammatical structures. The languages needn't be closely related: for instance, Italian and Russian both have endings after the verb to mark the person.

- Look for similarities between sounds, too. For example, the German *ü* is similar to the French short *u.*

KEY TERMS

Language transfer = the way in which a language you already know (e.g. English or German) affects another language you are learning (e.g. Danish).

Interference = mistakenly transferring a form from another language when the language you are learning uses a totally different form – e.g. saying an English *u* instead of a French *u;* or, in Spanish, writing the Italian word *burro* for 'butter' instead of the Spanish word *mantequilla* (in Spanish, *burro* means 'donkey'!).

Coping with interference

The key to coping with interference is not to worry too much – after all, the old language helps more than it hinders in the long run. Here are a few specific tips:

- If words in the wrong language keep coming up when you are trying to speak, it just means that using the old language is still more automatic for you. Get lots of speaking practice in the new language, doing your best to correct yourself each time this happens. Eventually, using the new language will become automatic as well.

- Meanwhile, even if you use an 'alien' word, it will often be close enough to be understood.

- To improve your accent, make your own pronunciation drill (▶ [S11] *Pronunciation drills*), focusing on the sounds where the old language is interfering.

- For problems with grammar, examine the problem areas one by one until you have a very clear understanding of the differences between the two systems. Rather than trying to keep the languages apart to avoid getting confused, it is often better to face the problem and learn them in parallel (e.g. 'English *to think OF* = Spanish *pensar EN* but French *penser A*'). Using a colour-coded system for highlighting the differences in your notebook may help (e.g. blue endings for French, orange for Spanish, and no highlighting where it's the same in both languages).

This is the end of the general-purpose part of this book, in which we have given advice and techniques on how to prepare and start learning. The last chapter of this section comprises a series of questionnaires that you may wish to complete in order to determine your learning profile and needs. Then, in Part 2, we give specific information and advice on six language areas and skills: vocabulary, grammar, reading, listening, writing and speaking.

5

Diagnostic questionnaires

This chapter contains a series of photocopiable questionnaires that will help you understand what type of learner you are, what you need to learn, and which learning strategies are likely to work best for you. These questionnaires are closely related to some of the issues discussed in different chapters of this book, as follows:

5.1 Learning style questionnaire

See Chapter 2, 'Learning style', p7.

5.2 Self-instruction aptitude questionnaire

See Chapter 2, 'Self-instruction aptitude', p10.

5.3 Self-instruction experience questionnaire

See Chapter 2, 'Self-instruction experience', p11.

5.4 Typical problems related to vocabulary

See Chapter 6.

5.5 Typical problems related to grammar

See Chapter 7.

5.6 Typical problems related to reading

See Chapter 8.

5.7 Typical problems related to listening

See Chapter 9.

5.8 Typical problems related to writing

See Chapter 10.

5.9 Typical problems related to speaking

See Chapter 11.

5.1 Learning style questionnaire

Answer the following ten questions by ticking the box that is nearest to your own experience:

1 When I read grammar explanations in coursebooks …
- ☐ A I usually find them difficult to understand
- ☐ B some I can follow, others I can't
- ☐ C I can usually understand and use them
- ☐ D (I haven't seen enough to judge)

2 When I see a grammar table …
- ☐ A I usually skip it
- ☐ B sometimes I skip it, other times I try to learn it
- ☐ C I usually try to learn it
- ☐ D I'm not sure what I usually do

3 I prefer to learn by …
- ☐ A talking with others rather than learning dry rules and word-lists
- ☐ B (I can learn either by talking to people or by studying the language)
- ☐ C getting a grammar and vocabulary base, then using the language
- ☐ D (I haven't enough experience to judge)

4 If I have a grounding in one language (e.g. Spanish) and then start a second language in the same family (e.g. Italian), the first language …
- ☐ A confuses me more than it helps
- ☐ B sometimes helps, sometimes confuses me
- ☐ C helps me more than it confuses me
- ☐ D (I have never tried to learn two languages in the same family)

5 If I hear or see a new word or phrase whose meaning I can't work out …
- ☐ A I usually don't worry about it
- ☐ B sometimes I look it up, at other times I don't worry about it
- ☐ C if possible, I usually look it up in a dictionary
- ☐ D (I haven't been in this situation)

6 If I hear or see a new word or phrase whose meaning I can guess at …
- ☐ A if possible, I try to use it when talking with a native speaker
- ☐ B sometimes I'll check it in a dictionary, sometimes I'll use it straight away
- ☐ C if possible, I try to check it in a dictionary before using it
- ☐ D (I don't guess word-meanings)

7 When talking to real-life native speakers whose language I only know a little bit …
- ☐ A I enjoy communicating with foreign words, gestures – everything!
- ☐ B I try to communicate, though it can be a bit scary or embarrassing at times
- ☐ C I find my lack of knowledge very embarrassing
- ☐ D (I've never met any real-life native speakers to talk to)

8 If I am about to do a task in the foreign country (e.g. reserve train tickets) and I don't know all the key words …
- ☐ A I usually just have a go and try to get the meaning across somehow
- ☐ B I sometimes stop to look them up in a dictionary or phrasebook, and sometimes just have a go
- ☐ C whenever possible, I quickly look them up in a dictionary or phrasebook
- ☐ D (I've never been in such a situation)

9 If, after doing such a task, I realise I made a very basic grammar or vocabulary mistake …
- ☐ A I don't worry about it
- ☐ B sometimes I make a mental note not to make that mistake again, at other times I don't worry
- ☐ C whenever possible, I make a mental note not to make that mistake again
- ☐ D (I've never been in such a situation)

10 Feedback on how my language-learning is going …
- ☐ A comes more from speaking with people than from tests and exercises
- ☐ B comes both from exercises and from how well I actually communicate
- ☐ C comes more from tests/exercises than from speaking with people
- ☐ D (I don't know)

Scores and profiles

To find your learning style, count up how many A answers you have, how many Bs, how many Cs and how many Ds. Enter the totals in the boxes below.

How many ...   **As?** ☐   **Bs?** ☐   **Cs?** ☐   **Ds?** ☐

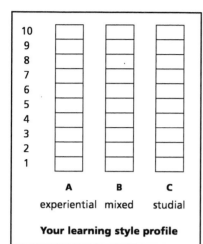

Your learning style profile

As are experiential answers, Bs are mixed-style answers, and Cs are studial answers. You can make your answers into a learning style profile by adding them to the chart below. If you had 5 As, shade in squares 1 to 5 (starting at the bottom) on the left-hand scale; if you had 3 Bs, shade in squares 1 to 3 on the middle scale; and if you had 2 Cs, shade in squares 1 to 2 on the right-hand scale. Leave the Ds for now.

Now look at your profile, and see which of the shapes below describes you best. If you are not sure which to choose, you are probably a mixed learner.

More experiential learners

You have a good number of As and very few if any Cs. Go back to Chapter 2, and read 'Experiential strengths and challenges' (p8).

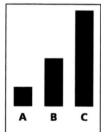

More studial learners

You have a good number of Cs and very few if any As. Go back to Chapter 2, and read 'Studial strengths and challenges' (p9).

Learners with a mixed learning style

You have a fairly balanced profile, with a good number of Bs. Go back to Chapter 2, and read 'Experiential strengths and challenges' (p8) and 'Studial strengths and challenges' (p9). Tick the features that apply to you, and follow the advice given for those features.

What if I have more Ds than anything else?

This shows that you are a less experienced learner. Most of the activities you use were probably suggested by your teachers, so they may not be a very good guide to your own learning style. This book as a whole will give you lots of activity ideas: try out as many as you can. In a few months, when you have tried out a range of activities, do the questionnaire again. For further details, see 'Self-instruction experience' (p11) and the Self-instruction experience questionnaire (p38).

5.2 Self-instruction aptitude questionnaire

Answer the following 10 questions by ticking the box that is nearest to your own experience. Be as honest as you can!

1 How good were you at foreign languages at school?
- ☐ A Quite/very good
- ☐ B Middling
- ☐ C Hopeless

2 If you had to learn an 'exotic' language like Arabic or Chinese, how would you regard the task?
- ☐ A As a fascinating challenge
- ☐ B As a chore, but probably not an impossible one
- ☐ C With terror

3 If you only have a smattering of a language, what do you do in the country where it is spoken?
- ☐ A Have fun trying out what I've got
- ☐ B Use the language if I have to
- ☐ C Ask 'do you speak English?', or rely on friends who speak it well

4 Are you good at imitating voices and accents in your own language?
- ☐ A People say I'm a good mimic
- ☐ B It depends on the voice or accent
- ☐ C No

5 If you can understand the gist of what a native speaker is saying in a foreign language, but not certain key words, what do you do?
- ☐ A I don't worry: as long as something gets through, that's fine
- ☐ B Try to puzzle out the key words
- ☐ C Panic

6 How easily distracted are you (in general)?
- ☐ A Once I've started a job, I'm dead to the world
- ☐ B It depends on what I'm doing
- ☐ C Very

7 If you have a number of major jobs to do at once (not necessarily language learning), what do you do?
- ☐ A Plan my time so that they all get done
- ☐ B Get most of them done somehow, though not to any pre-set plan
- ☐ C Get in a tizzy

8 If you set yourself a goal that involves learning a new skill (not necessarily a language), do you stick to it?
- ☐ A If the goal is realistic, I usually stick to it
- ☐ B Sometimes
- ☐ C I tend to give up once the first enthusiasm wears off

9 If you are teaching yourself a new skill, how often do you practise or work at it?
- ☐ A Nearly every day
- ☐ B Reasonably regularly, though other things can get in the way
- ☐ C When I feel like it

10 How easy would it be to find half an hour's 'quiet time' a day for language learning?
- ☐ A I could find the time without disrupting my life
- ☐ B Possible, but I'd have to sacrifice something else
- ☐ C Impossible: my life is already too full!

Scoring

To find your Self-Instruction Aptitude score, give yourself 2 points for every A answer, 1 point for every B, and 0 points for every C. Add up your total score, and enter it in the box below.

Total self-instruction aptitude score

If you scored **0–5**   you have a **low** Self-Instruction Aptitude score.

If you scored **6–14**   you have a **medium** Self-Instruction Aptitude score.

If you scored **15–20** you have a **high** Self-Instruction Aptitude score.

Now go back to Chapter 2 ('Self-instruction aptitude', p10) and read the information in the appropriate box for your score.

5.3 Self-instruction experience questionnaire

Answer the following 10 questions by ticking the box that is nearest to your own experience. Be as honest as you can!

1 In how many foreign languages do you have at least some experience of teaching yourself (instead of or as well as classwork)?

☐ A None

☐ B One

☐ C Two or more

2 In how many languages have you worked on your own with a teach-yourself course?

☐ A None

☐ B One

☐ C Two or more

3 How many languages have you deliberately tried to improve using real-life materials, such as videos, magazines, radio/TV, etc?

☐ A None

☐ B One

☐ C Two or more

4 What is the highest level you have ever reached in a foreign language without a teacher?

☐ A No experience, or I've tried but failed to get anywhere

☐ B A smattering: basic words and phrases only

☐ C Able to survive reasonably or very well in the language

5 Have you ever used self-instruction after getting at least a basic knowledge from a classroom course?

☐ A No

☐ B Yes, but I've only used self-instruction while following a class

☐ C Yes: I've switched to self-instruction instead of continuing a class

6 Have you any teach-yourself experience (with or without a classwork basis) in a 'difficult European' (Celtic, Slavic, Greek, Hungarian, etc) or non-European language?

☐ A No

☐ B I've tried but not got very far

☐ C Yes, and I've reached elementary level or higher

7 Look back at the Learning style questionnaire (p35).

In the box here, write how many D answers you got.

Scoring

To find your Language experience score:

- For **Questions 1–6**, score 2 points for every A answer, 1 point for every B answer and 0 points for every C answer.

- For **Question 7**, your points score is the number you wrote in the box.

Add up your total score, and enter it in the box below.

If your total score is:

Total experience score

- **0–7** you are a **Veteran** teach-yourself learner. Look at box V in 'Self-instruction experience' (p11).

- **8–15** you are a **Fully-Fledged** teach-yourself learner. Look at box F in 'Self-instruction experience' (p11).

- **16–22** you are a **Novice** teach-yourself learner. Look at box N in 'Self-instruction experience' (p11).

5.4 Typical problems related to vocabulary

	Page
DIY SOLUTIONS	
[V] Chapter 6 (Vocabulary)	53
[G] Chapter 7 (Grammar)	62
[R] Chapter 8 (Reading)	70
[W] Chapter 9 (Listening)	86
[L] Chapter 10 (Writing)	99
[S] Chapter 11 (Speaking)	118

The rest of this chapter gives a set of ready-references to the DIY techniques in Part 2. There are three ways of accessing strategies for improving your vocabulary:

1 Read Chapter 6 through and tick the strategies which you feel would help.

2 Use the questionnaire below: tick the vocabulary problems which apply to you, and then look up the suggested 'DIY solutions' in the appropriate chapter.

References to Part 1 are shown by section titles. If you are focusing on vocabulary, we also advise you to read 'What does learning vocabulary involve?' (p53), as this will give you useful background information.

3 Refer to the alphabetical list at the back of the book.

Problems		**DIY solutions**		**Page**
☐ **1**	I find it really difficult to remember new words.	**[V1]**	*Word map*	56
		[V2]	*Word table*	57
		[V3]	*Made-up sentences*	58
		[V4]	*Word lists*	58
		[V5]	*Labelled objects*	59
		[V6]	*Papers in a hat*	60
		[V7]	*Crosswords*	60
		[V8]	*Anagrams*	61
		[G6]	*Chop and jumble*	67
☐ **2**	I can't recognise words that I know when I hear them in continuous speech.	**[L8]**	*Using a transcript*	91
☐ **3**	I just don't know enough general vocabulary to feel comfortable with speaking, reading, listening or writing in the foreign language.	**[V1]**	*Word map*	56
		[V2]	*Word table*	57
		[V3]	*Made-up sentences*	58
		[V4]	*Word lists*	58
		[V5]	*Labelled objects*	59
		[V6]	*Papers in a hat*	60
		[V7]	*Crosswords*	60
		[V8]	*Anagrams*	61
		[G6]	*Chop and jumble*	67
☐ **4**	I need to learn enough vocabulary to cope with a particular topic (e.g. my specialist subject, my favourite hobby) or in a particular situation (e.g. registering for a course, talking to a potential customer).		'Using a dictionary'	27
		[R7]	*Predicting words in a text*	77
		[L11]	*Predicting words in a recording*	93
		[S3]	*Creating a role play*	123

☐	**5**	I generally know the words that I would need, but I can never recall them fast enough when I have to speak.	**[S6]**	*Imaginary chats*	126
			[G8]	*Learn it by heart*	68
☐	**6**	I know the words, but I tend to use them in the wrong context.	**[V3]**	*Made-up sentences*	58
			[G6]	*Chop and jumble*	67
				'Using a dictionary'	27
☐	**7**	I can remember the actual words, but not their spelling.	**[V7]**	*Crosswords*	60
			[V8]	*Anagrams*	61
☐	**8**	I can remember the actual words, but not their gender, declension, conjugation etc.	**[V3]**	*Made-up sentences*	58
			[G6]	*Chop and jumble*	67
			[W2]	*Back translation*	102
				'Using a dictionary'	27
☐	**9**	I tend to use words in the wrong order or with the wrong preposition.	**[V3]**	*Made-up sentences*	58
			[G6]	*Chop and jumble*	67
			[W2]	*Back translation*	102
				'Using a dictionary'	27
☐	**10**	I tend to remember roughly what words sound or look like, but I often come up with something that only vaguely resembles the intended word. This can cause embarrassing misunderstandings at times.	**[V7]**	*Crosswords*	60
			[V8]	*Anagrams*	61
			[W2]	*Back translation*	102
☐	**11**	Sometimes when I use the right words I don't get understood because of my pronunciation	**[S10]**	*Listen and repeat*	129
			[S11]	*Pronunciation drills*	129
			[S12]	*Reading aloud*	130
☐	**12**	I keep getting this language mixed up with another foreign language that I learnt in the past.		'Using related languages'	32

5.5 Typical problems related to grammar

There are four ways of accessing strategies for improving your grammar:

1   Read Chapter 7 through and tick the strategies which you feel would help.

2   Use the questionnaire below: tick the grammar problems which apply to you, and then look up the suggested 'DIY solutions' in the appropriate chapter:

References to Part 1 are shown by section title. If you are focusing on grammar, we also advise you to read 'What does learning grammar involve?' (p62), as this will give you useful background information.

3   You may also wish to look at 'Typical problems related to writing' (p47), as many of the problems experienced when writing are grammar-related.

4   Refer to the alphabetical list at the back of the book.

Problems		DIY solutions	Page
☐ **1**	I don't know the grammar in my own language, let alone the foreign language!	'Choosing a grammar book'	29
		[G7] *Finding examples*	68
☐ **2**	My knowledge of grammar in the foreign language is absolutely terrible. I lack a solid foundation.	'Choosing a grammar book'	29
		[W2] *Back translation*	102
		[W16] *Marking your written performance*	113
☐ **3**	Another foreign language keeps interfering.	'Using related languages'	32
☐ **4**	I have been learning grammar rules for a while, yet I often don't understand my mistakes. It all seems very confusing.	'Choosing a grammar book'	29
		[G9] *Seeking feedback*	69
☐ **5**	My knowledge of grammar is patchy, but I'm not sure what the most serious gaps might be.	[W2] *Back translation* (to identify problem areas)	102
		'Choosing a grammar book'	29
		[G9] *Seeking feedback*	69
☐ **6**	I have a pretty good idea of my basic problems with the grammar of this language. I just need a method to tackle them.	[G3] *Getting rid of known mistakes*	66
☐ **7**	I learnt the language by talking to native speakers rather than through study. As a result, my language is understandable, but full of mistakes.	[G5] *Self-transcript*	67
		[W1] *Editing a transcript*	102
		[W2] *Back translation*	102
		[G9] *Seeking feedback*	69

☐ **8** I know I need to improve my grammar, but it's
just so boring to learn it!

[W3]	*Creating a gapped text*	103
[G6]	*Chop and jumble*	67
[G5]	*Self-transcript*	67
[G4]	*Teaching a rule*	66
[W2]	*Back translation*	102

☐ **9** I know some basic grammar, but I need to learn
the rest.

	'Choosing a grammar book'	29
[G4]	*Teaching a rule*	66
[G9]	*Seeking feedback*	69

☐ **10** I do know a few/many rules, but I just can't apply
grammar when I am talking.

[G3]	*Getting rid of known mistakes*	66
[G5]	*Self-transcript*	67
[G9]	*Seeking feedback*	69

5.6 Typical problems related to reading

There are three ways of accessing strategies for improving your reading:

1 Read Chapter 8 through and tick the strategies which you feel would help.

2 Use the questionnaire below: tick the reading problems which apply to you, and then look up the suggested 'DIY solutions' in the appropriate chapter.

References to Part 1 are shown by section titles. If you are focusing on reading, we also advise you to read 'What does learning to read in a foreign language involve?' (p70), as this will give you useful background information.

3 Refer to the alphabetical list at the back of the book.

Problems		DIY solutions	Page
☐ **1**	I am still very slow deciphering the foreign script (for languages using a different script).	**[R3]** *Learning a new script*	74
☐ **2**	I have problems reading in any language because my eyesight is poor.	**[R4]** *Improving visual perception*	75
☐ **3**	I have problems reading in any language because I am dyslexic.	**[W8]** *Tips for dyslexic learners* **[R1]** *Basic reading strategies* **[R4]** *Improving visual perception*	107 72 75
☐ **4**	I'm just not a great reader, even in my own language.	**[R1]** *Basic reading strategies* **[R8]** *Text collections* **[R16]** *Surfing the Net* **[R14]** *Recall techniques for reading* **[R18]** *Timed reading* **[R13]** *Highlighting*	72 78 83 82 85 81
☐ **5**	I don't normally understand enough words to even get the gist of what I am reading.	**[R2]** *Choosing a text* All Vocabulary learning techniques (Chapter 6)	73
☐ **6**	I can generally get the gist, but I miss out most of the detail.	**[R6]** *Intensive reading* **[R15]** *Asking questions about a text*	77 82
☐ **7**	I can get most of the meaning, but I'm sure I don't get the subtle nuances conveyed through style, humour, etc.	**[R5]** *Extensive reading* **[L10]** *Extensive listening* **[L6]** *Observing native speakers*	76 93 90
☐ **8**	I am constantly looking up words in the dictionary. It does slow me down, but I want to know what the words mean.	**[R1]** *Basic reading strategies* **[R5]** *Extensive reading* **[R13]** *Highlighting*	72 76 81

☐ **9**	When I am reading, I only look up key words. These are the only ones I might try to memorise.	**[R6]** *Intensive reading*	77

☐ **10**	I don't like to interrupt my reading in order to look up words in the dictionary, so I just read on even if I miss out entire paragraphs.	**[R6]** *Intensive reading*	77
		[R15] *Asking questions on a text*	82

☐ **11**	I find it difficult to know whether a text is suitable for my level.	**[R2]** *Choosing a text*	73

☐ **12**	I don't know where to find texts that are suitable for my level.	**[R2]** *Choosing a text*	73
		[R16] *Surfing the Net*	83

☐ **13**	I need to be able to read a particular kind of text related to my work/my study/my personal interests.	**[R10]** *Predicting questions in a text*	80
		[R7] *Predicting words in a text*	77
		[R8] *Text collections*	78

☐ **14**	I want to widen my vocabulary through reading practice.	**[R6]** *Intensive reading*	77
		[R7] *Predicting words in a text*	77
		[R8] *Text collections*	78
		(Use these in combination with the vocabulary learning techniques described in Chapter 6.)	

☐ **15**	I want to improve my grammar through reading practice.	**[R11]** *Coffee stains*	80
		[R17] *Hybrid texts*	84
		[G6] *Chop and jumble*	67
		[G7] *Finding examples*	68
		[W3] *Creating a gapped text*	103

☐ **16**	I just want to improve my general language skills through reading practice.	All the techniques in Chapter 8, though see especially:	
		[R8] *Text collections*	78
		[R9] *Text reviews*	79
		[R12] *Comparing media*	81
		[R5] *Extensive reading*	76
		[R6] *Intensive reading*	77

5.7 Typical problems related to listening

There are three ways of accessing strategies for improving your listening:

DIY SOLUTIONS

	Page
[V] Chapter 6 (Vocabulary)	53
[G] Chapter 7 (Grammar)	62
[R] Chapter 8 (Reading)	70
[W] Chapter 9 (Listening)	86
[L] Chapter 10 (Writing)	99
[S] Chapter 11 (Speaking)	118

1 Read Chapter 9 through and tick the strategies which you feel would help.

2 Use the questionnaire below: tick the listening problems which apply to you, and then look up the suggested 'DIY Solutions' in the appropriate chapter.

References to Part 1 are shown by section titles. If you are focusing on listening, we also advise you to read 'What does learning to listen to a foreign language involve?' (p86), as this will give you useful background information.

3 Refer to the alphabetical list at the back of the book.

Problems		**DIY solutions**		**Page**
☐ **1**	Listening always makes me very anxious.	**[L1]**	*Listening for beginners*	88
		[L8]	*Using a transcript*	91
		[L3]	*Joint listening*	89
☐ **2**	My hearing is not very good, so listening is more difficult for me than for other people.	**[L2]**	*Improving perception*	88
		[L4]	*Tandem listening*	89
		[L3]	*Joint listening*	89
☐ **3**	I can't work out where one word ends and the next one begins. It's all a slurred flow of incomprehensible sounds.	**[L8]**	*Using a transcript*	91
		[L4]	*Tandem listening*	89
		[L3]	*Joint listening*	89
☐ **4**	I can't even recognise words that I am supposed to know when these are spoken at normal speed.	**[L8]**	*Using a transcript*	91
		[L4]	*Tandem listening*	89
		[L3]	*Joint listening*	89
☐ **5**	I'm generally OK with specially recorded listening tasks that are intended for my level, but authentic speech is extremely difficult.	**[L1]**	*Listening for beginners*	88
		[L9]	*Asking questions about a recording*	92
☐ **6**	I just don't know the language well enough to understand what is being said.	**[L1]**	*Listening for beginners*	88
			(See also the vocabulary learning techniques described in Chapter 6)	
☐ **7**	I'm generally OK when people are talking to me, but I can't understand native speakers when they are talking among themselves.	**[L6]**	*Observing native speakers*	90
		[L4]	*Tandem listening*	89

☐ **8**	I'm generally OK with formal speech (e.g. general news reports), but I find colloquial speech extremely difficult to understand.	**[L4]**	*Tandem listening*	89
		[L5]	*Recording native speakers*	90
☐ **9**	I'm generally OK with everyday speech (especially if I can ask to repeat), but I find formal speech (e.g. news reports, lectures, etc) very difficult to understand.	**[L12]**	*Note-taking*	94
		[L7]	*Writing a transcript*	91
		[L9]	*Asking questions about a recording*	92
☐ **10**	I need to be able to act as an interpreter between two speakers of different languages.	**[L13]**	*Prepared listening*	95
		[S13]	*Shadowing*	130
		[L15]	*Recall techniques for listening*	97
☐ **11**	I need to be able to understand academic lectures in the foreign language.	**[L12]**	*Note-taking*	94
		[L7]	*Writing a transcript*	91
		[L13]	*Prepared listening*	95
☐ **12**	I'm generally OK if the speakers have a familiar accent, but I need to learn to understand other accents (or one accent in particular).	**[L14]**	*Unfamiliar accents*	96
		[L7]	*Writing a transcript*	91
		[L8]	*Using a transcript*	91
		[L5]	*Recording native speakers*	90
☐ **13**	I have access to foreign language programmes on satellite TV, but I don't know how to use them for improving my language skills.	**[L16]**	*Using satellite TV*	98
		[L11]	*Predicting words in a recording*	93
		[L10]	*Extensive listening*	93
		[L1]	*Listening for beginners*	88
		[L15]	*Recall techniques for listening*	97
☐ **14**	I just need to improve my general listening comprehension skills.	**[L9]**	*Asking questions about a recording*	92
		[L4]	*Tandem listening*	89
		[L3]	*Joint listening*	89
		[L5]	*Recording native speakers*	90
		[L15]	*Recall techniques for listening*	97

5.8 Typical problems related to writing

There are three ways of accessing strategies for improving your writing:

	DIY SOLUTIONS	
		Page
[V]	Chapter 6 (Vocabulary)	53
[G]	Chapter 7 (Grammar)	62
[R]	Chapter 8 (Reading)	70
[W]	Chapter 9 (Listening)	86
[L]	Chapter 10 (Writing)	99
[S]	Chapter 11 (Speaking)	118

1 Read Chapter 10 through and tick the strategies which you feel would help.

2 Use the questionnaire below: tick the writing problems which apply to you, and then look up the suggested 'DIY solutions' in the appropriate chapter.

References to Part 1 are shown by section titles. If you are focusing on writing, we also advise you to read 'What does writing in a foreign language involve?' (p99), as this will give you useful background information.

3 Refer to the alphabetical list at the back of the book.

Problems		**DIY solutions**	**Page**
☐ **1**	I just can't write without constantly referring to my dictionary.	See the vocabulary learning techniques described in Chapter 6.	
☐ **2**	My grammar is terrible, to such an extent that what I write is often incomprehensible.	**[W2]** *Back translation*	102
		[R5] *Extensive reading*	76
		[R6] *Intensive reading*	77
		See also the grammar learning techniques described in Chapter 7.	
☐ **3**	My spelling is terrible, but I can generally be understood.	**[V8]** *Anagrams*	61
		[V7] *Crosswords*	60
		[W2] *Back translation* (*)	102
		[W11] *Dictation* (*)	109
		(*) Try to have these checked by somebody else!	
☐ **4**	Writing is difficult in any language because I am dyslexic.	**[W8]** *Tips for dyslexic learners*	107
		See also:	
		[W12] *Joint writing*	110
		[W10] *Letters and e-mail*	109
		[R16] *Surfing the Net*	83
☐ **5**	I can only write in very simple sentences.	**[W5]** *Paragraph expansion*	105
		[W4] *Linking sentences and paragraphs*	103
☐ **6**	I try to write complex sentences sometimes, but the results are often unsuccessful.	**[W9]** *Writing a pastiche*	108
		[W3] *Creating a gapped text* (using link words/expressions as gaps)	103
		[G8] *Learn it by heart*	68

☐	**7**	I keep making the same mistakes all the time.	**[G3]**	*Getting rid of known mistakes*	66
			[W3]	*Creating a gapped text* (using problem areas as gaps, e.g. word endings, verbs, particles …)	103
			[W16]	*Marking your written performance*	113
☐	**8**	I often pick up the wrong word in my dictionary.		'Using a dictionary'	27
			[W16]	*Marking your written performance*	113
☐	**9**	I often write words in the wrong order.	**[G6]**	*Chop and jumble*	67
			[W2]	*Back translation*	102
☐	**10**	My writing is OK, but I would like to improve my style.	**[W6]**	*Rewriting a text*	105
			[W9]	*Writing a pastiche*	108
			[R8]	*Text collections* based on	78
				[R6] *Intensive reading* and	77
				[R5] *Extensive reading*	77
☐	**11**	I am OK with grammar exercises, but it all goes out of the window when I write a proper text.	**[W12]**	*Joint writing*	110
			[W10]	*Letters and e-mail*	109
			[W14]	*Keeping a diary*	111
			[W13]	*Songs and poems*	111
			[R5]	*Extensive reading*	76
☐	**12**	I need to learn how to write a particular kind of text (e.g. CVs, information requests, academic papers, etc).	**[W9]**	*Writing a pastiche*	108
			[R8]	*Text collections,* based on	78
				[R6] *Intensive reading* of the type of text required.	77
			[W15]	*Written project work*	112

5.9 Typical problems related to speaking

DIY SOLUTIONS

There are three ways of accessing strategies for improving your speaking:

1 Read Chapter 11 through and tick the strategies which you feel would help.

2 Use the questionnaire below: tick the speaking problems which apply to you, and then look up the suggested 'DIY solutions' in the appropriate chapter.

References to Part 1 are shown by section titles. If you are focusing on speaking, we also advise you to read 'What does speaking in a foreign language involve?' (p118), as this will give you useful background information.

3 Refer to the alphabetical list at the back of the book.

Problems	DIY solutions	Page
☐ **1** I really need to do something about my accent/I need to improve stress and intonation.	**[S11]** *Pronunciation drills*	129
	[S10] *Listen and repeat*	129
	[S13] *Shadowing* (for advanced level only)	130
	[S12] *Reading aloud*	130
	[S7] *Learning a song*	127
☐ **2** I just don't know enough words to say what I want to say.	**[V1]** *Word map*	56
	[V2] *Word table*	57
	[V3] *Made-up sentences*	58
	[V7] *Crosswords*	60
	[V8] *Anagrams*	61
	[V4] *Word lists*	58
	[V5] *Labelled objects*	59
	[V6] *Papers in a hat*	60
	[G6] *Chop and jumble*	67
☐ **3** I may know the words I need, but I find it difficult to recall them when I am speaking.		
☐ **4** I manage to say a couple of well-prepared sentences, but then I get stuck.	**[S3]** *Creating a role play*	123
	[S6] *Imaginary chats*	126
	[G8] *Learn it by heart*	68
☐ **5** It takes me forever to get a sentence out.	Plus the vocabulary learning techniques described in Chapter 6.	
☐ **6** I have no significant problems when I write, but speaking is really a struggle.		
☐ **7** In real conversations, I don't get a chance to speak. By the time I work out what I am going to say, the conversation has moved on.	Turn-taking strategies:	
	[L6] *Observing native speakers*	90
	[S8] *Interrupting your partner*	127
	[S9] *Outspeaking your partner*	128

	8	I'm just terribly shy. I don't even like talking to strangers in my own language!	Graded confidence-building tasks:	
			[S10] *Listen and repeat*	129
			[S6] *Imaginary chats*	126
			[S4] *Recording yourself*	124
			[S5] *Tandem ice-breakers*	125

	9	I can manage to get my ideas across, but my language is terrible.	**[G5]** *Self-transcript*	67
			See also the other grammar learning techniques described in Chapter 7.	

	10	I can't say a sentence unless I feel reasonably sure that it is grammatically correct.	**[L10]** *Extensive listening,* using authentic material (avoid intensive listening and work involving transcripts for the moment).	93
			[S5] *Tandem ice-breakers*	125
			[G8] *Learn it by heart*	68

	11	I feel very anxious when I have to talk on the phone.	Make a glossary of useful 'telephone' phrases using the **[V4]** *Word lists* technique.	58
			[S3] *Creating a role play*	123
			[S2] *Don't look!*	122
			[L5] *Recording native speakers* (simulating a telephone conversation), followed by	90
			[S10] *Listen and repeat* and	129
			[G8] *Learn it by heart* (all using the same telephone conversation).	68

	12	I am reasonably fluent, but I get the feeling that the way in which I say things doesn't quite sound 'right' (or doesn't get the expected reaction from my native conversation partners).		
			If your problem is mostly with stress and intonation:	
			[L6] *Observing native speakers* (or	90
			[L5] *Recording native speakers*), followed by	90
			[S10] *Listen and repeat*	129
			or	
			[S13] *Shadowing* (using the same recording for all).	130
			If your problem is the type of language that you use:	
			[S4] *Recording yourself* and	124
			[G5] *Self-transcript,* followed by discussion of any inappropriacies with a native speaker.	67

part

2

DIY
techniques

chapter 6

Vocabulary

What does learning vocabulary involve?

Vocabulary is the most crucial element of language. Without grammar you can get by in a foreign language: 'Station, please?' is perfectly understandable. But without vocabulary items (i.e. individual words and standard phrases, such as *money*, *pocket money*, *put your money where your mouth is*, etc), you can communicate nothing. This means that effective vocabulary strategies are vital both for learning foreign-language vocabulary and for coping with situations where you don't know all the words. But first, what does 'learning vocabulary' actually mean?

How much vocabulary?

The main problem with vocabulary is that there is so much of it to learn. Estimates of how many words the average native speaker knows vary enormously. One guess says that 'only' about 3,000 words are used in everyday conversation, but that the educated reader can recognise up to ten times as many. So how many do you need to know in a foreign language? Studies have shown that the minimum survival level for everyday reading and conversation is about 2,000 words, and a 'good' command of a foreign language probably means at least 5,000 words. The first level, i.e. the 2,000-word survival threshold, is the vital one and should be your key goal when starting a new language. Getting there also boosts motivation, for once you are actually able to read shop-signs or newspaper headlines, and talk to native speakers, you can see that all your hard work has paid off at last!

How long it should take to get to survival level depends on several factors. The main ones are the amount of work you put in, and whether or not the language is related to one you know well. Assuming five learning sessions a week, an English native speaker with GCSE French might take a year to get to survival level in Spanish, say; but Japanese could take two or three times as long, especially if she was learning to write as well as speak.

Patterns of vocabulary

In our brain, the vocabulary items we know are linked together into logical networks. Here are some of the most important:

- **Semantic field.** Words and phrases are related to a common theme, such as eating out (*waiter, table, soup, overcooked, bill*) or emotions (*love, like, hate, wonderful*).

- **Sound group.** Words and phrases have sounds in common, e.g. *glee, glug, glamour*; or *wonderful, beautiful, bashful*.

- **Word family.** Words and phrases have the same etymological root, e.g. *common, commonwealth, commune, community, communal*.

- **Emotional pattern.** 'Words that make me feel nostalgic' or 'words I hate'.

- **Associations.** Words and phrases that have personal links: e.g. *grandmother, fish and chips, Yorkshire*.

Each item belongs to several different types of network at once. When we want to call it up from memory in order to use it in conversation (e.g. *Auntie May*), our brain chooses a probable pattern it belongs to (e.g. distant relatives) and starts searching along the network. If the search fails, another network may be tried, e.g. sound (*Auntie M* ...) or associations (e.g. blue hat, Uncle George's funeral).

If this is how items are stored, it makes sense to organise your foreign-language learning according to these networks. For example, a semantic field-based method might involve reading an illustrated magazine article on home furnishings, noting down new vocabulary, and next day covering over the text and trying to write a description of the picture. Depending on learning style, however, different learners may well prefer different patterns (grouping words into word families, say, will appeal more to studial than to experiential learners).

Vocabulary learning

Knowing foreign-language vocabulary involves both remembering it (i.e. storing it in memory), and being able to use it (i.e. get it out of memory) quickly and effortlessly. Here are a few key facts about remembering:

- The more 'attention', i.e. brain power, we devote to an item, the more likely we are to remember it (this is why we soon remember foreign-language words that sound like dirty words in our mother tongue!).

- But after more than about twenty minutes, our brain gets so tired of doing high-attention tasks (e.g. repeating a word-list) that it stops paying attention. So, change activities every twenty minutes, and wait at least a few hours before repeating the same learning task. Or do a low-attention task, e.g. flick through a foreign-language magazine.

- In these twenty minutes, you can give a few items a lot of attention, or a lot of items a little bit of attention.

However, the first time you 'remember' an item, it's very likely to be forgotten again; but the more separate learning sessions you devote to an item, the less likely you are to forget it. This why a once-a-day routine works so well for many learners.

Here are a few activities that help remembering, with their pros and cons:

ACTIVITY	PROS	CONS
Listening (films, radio) or reading (books, magazines).	Low attention (if you can understand the general gist), so no twenty-minute time limit ...	... but a lot of sessions needed before items are remembered.
	Fun ...	High attention if the text is difficult.
	Items are in real-life context, so can more easily be used.	Can be hard to find texts for beginner/elementary learners.
Repeating (dialogues, etc)	Gives items in realistic sentence context.	
	Medium-attention: easy ...	... but takes more sessions.
Word-lists: guessing items from mother tongue equivalents.	High-attention: quite effective ...	... but quite tiring.
		No context, so realistic practice is also needed.
Keyword-imagery: making silly puns – e.g. French *mère* sounds like a mother horse (mare).	Very high attention: very effective ...	... but very tiring.
		Can often be difficult to think of a pun.

As for being able to use what you have remembered, the technique is quite simple: **practice,** and lots of it. Practice should be as realistic as possible: just as you only learn how to drive by driving, so you only learn to speak to people by speaking to people. Note, by the way, that spoken and written sounds of a word are stored differently (as any learner of Chinese or Japanese can tell you!), and that being able to recognise a word isn't the same as being able to use it. This means that, whichever of **the four language skills** (listening, speaking, reading and writing) you need to develop, you will have to work on them separately: so, if you need to learn written vocabulary, you'll have to practise writing it.

Finally, remember that **variety** is the spice of learning. The more ways that you tackle the same set of vocabulary items (e.g. repeating word-lists, translating, reading in texts, using in conversations, etc), the faster and the more effectively you are likely to learn them.

TECHNIQUES

The rest of this chapter gives a step-by-step description of all the techniques suggested for vocabulary learning.

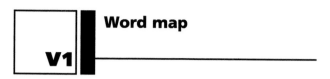

Word map

What is it good for?

Areas of vocabulary in which you have only basic knowledge and want to expand. Step 4 below (labelling the arrows **between** different items) is particularly important, as it draws your attention to necessary words that would be overlooked in conventional vocabulary searches.

How to proceed

Choose a topic and write down as many words as you can remember in relation to the topic (or get a competent speaker to give you a quick list off the top of his/her head).

1   Draw up the main word in the centre of a blank page (as the word 'book' in the example below).

2   Arrange the other words around it. Use a dictionary to fill any obvious gaps in the diagram (▶ 'Using a dictionary', p27).

3   Draw up a series of arrows showing the links between the different words.

4   If most of your words are nouns, label the arrows with the relevant verbs, so that you can make sentences as you 'travel' through the network (for instance in this example: 'the **author** writes the **book**').

How to assess progress

- If you can, get a competent speaker to check through all the links that you have labelled.

- Photocopy your diagram and tippex the words from most of the boxes (or simply copy it by hand leaving some blanks). Try to complete it a few days later.

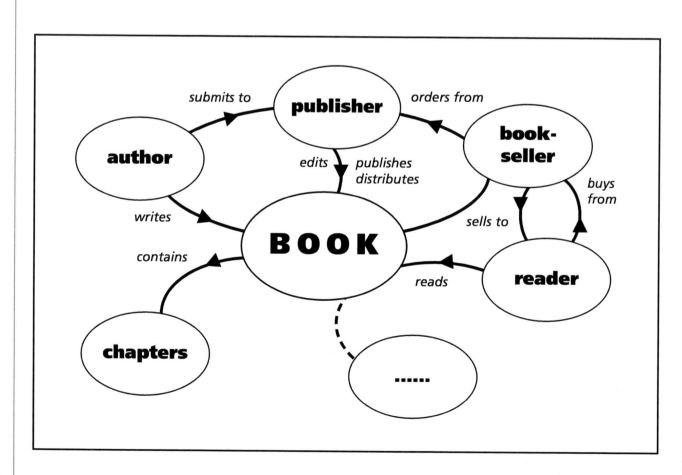

Word table

V2

What is it good for?

For vocabulary areas in which you have only basic knowledge and where you feel you need to expand and cover more nuances.

How to proceed

1 Choose a topic and write down as many words as you can find in relation to the topic (or get a competent speaker to give you a quick list off the top of his/her head).

2 Make a table with a column for each specific feature that makes any difference between the meaning of related words. Use a good monolingual dictionary (▶ 'Choosing a dictionary', p25) or consult a competent speaker if you are unsure about a particular nuance.

The example below shows nouns for 'things to sit on', but you can also use verbs (e.g. 'moving from A to B': *run, walk, jump ...*) or adjectives ('pleasant feelings': *happy, pleased, delighted ...*).

How to assess progress

• If you can, get a competent speaker to check through your table.

• A few days later, cover over the column which has the words and try to remember which word was which using only the list of features.

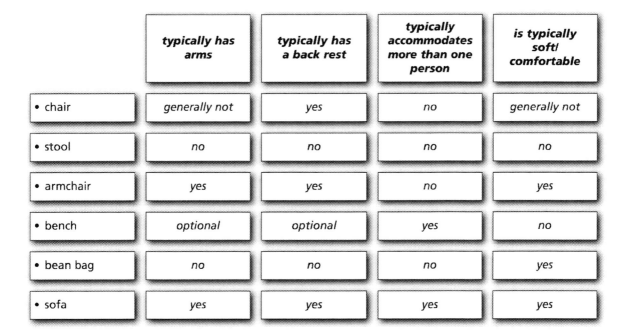

	typically has arms	*typically has a back rest*	*typically accommodates more than one person*	*is typically soft/ comfortable*
• chair	*generally not*	*yes*	*no*	*generally not*
• stool	*no*	*no*	*no*	*no*
• armchair	*yes*	*yes*	*no*	*yes*
• bench	*optional*	*optional*	*yes*	*no*
• bean bag	*no*	*no*	*no*	*yes*
• sofa	*yes*	*yes*	*yes*	*yes*

Made-up sentences

V3

What is it good for?

Learning a word is not only about remembering the actual word in isolation. You must also learn the context in which it can be used and the grammatical rules that are related to it (correct word order, any prepositions or other words that typically occur with it, etc).

How to proceed

1 Make up sentences containing the words you want to learn. You may include more than one new word in the sentences. Try to make them into a story (note that funny or absurd stories are easier to remember than sensible ones!).

2 If you are not absolutely sure that all your sentences are correct, have them checked by somebody who is more proficient than you in the language.

3 Learn them by heart, using your favourite memory technique (▶ 'Memorisation techniques', p30).

How to assess progress

The best way to assess the results is to try and use the new words in conversation at the earliest opportunity (▶ **[V9]** *Recycling*).

Word lists

V4

What is it good for?

Word lists are the most popular technique for learning new vocabulary. There are many ways to go about it, and also a few precautions to be taken.

Basic precautions

1 Don't leave out any information that you might need later:

- In languages where words have a gender, write down the correct article in front of the word (or an abbreviation of its gender, or even colour-coding) and learn it at the same time.

- If a verb is irregular, write down the specific verb forms that you need to know in order to use it correctly.

- If a word always requires a certain preposition, a particular case, etc, write it down and learn it at the same time.

- If the pronunciation is not obvious, make a note of it along with the word.

- In languages which use accents or any other symbols, don't ever leave these out and make sure that you learn them as part of the words.

2 Stick to the meanings that you are sure about:

- Because sentences in a foreign language are hardly ever word-for-word translations of their English equivalent, it is always a good idea to learn words in context. Try to remember them within sentences rather than by themselves (▶ **[V3]** *Made-up sentences*, **[G7]** *Finding examples*).

- Just because one word means something in English, it doesn't necessarily mean exactly the same in the foreign language (e.g. *'a nail'* in a hand vs. *'a nail'* that you hit with a hammer). Add 'meaning notes' to narrow down the definition to what you are sure about.

3 Don't overdo it!

It's easy to get obsessed by word lists, but if it isn't backed by other methods (e.g. reading, speaking), you can quickly forget what you have memorised.

Labelled objects

How to proceed

1 *Writing your list* – Basically, a good word list is one that works for you. Here are a few ideas:

- Alphabetic lists (by first letter only).

- Words related to the same semantic field (or 'topic').

- Words sharing a grammatical rule (e.g. irregular verbs that are similar, nouns belonging to the same gender, declension, etc).

- Words sharing a common stem ('word families').

- Words containing a particular sound.

- Words that you first saw/heard in a particular text, recording or real-life situation.

2 *Adding translations* – People usually add translations opposite the target language word, but you don't have to.

3 *Multiple lists* – The more things you do with a word, the more likely you are to remember it. Try to re-arrange the same set of words in several different ways. You can use some of the ideas listed above.

How to assess progress

A tried and tested method is to write the words in two columns, one in the target language, the other in your mother tongue. Test yourself by covering up one side, then repeat the test covering the other side. You could also tick off the words that you already know in order to focus only on those that are still a problem. Remember: little and often is best!

What is it good for?

This is a good technique for memorising new words through repeated exposure in your everyday routine. It is best suited to learning the names of objects or rooms used in everyday life. However, with a bit of imagination, you can also use the technique to learn other words, so long as you are able to associate these with a particular place or with an object in your daily environment.

How to proceed

- For nouns of everyday objects, write the words you want to learn on the relevant objects around the house.

- For other words, write labels with the words you want to learn and stick them in different rooms around the house. Imagine yourself following different paths and finding the things that those words refer to. E.g. to learn the names of wild animals, imagine that you have put a giraffe in the bedroom, a hippopotamus in the bath, a penguin in the fridge and a lion in the living room!

How to assess progress

Stage 1: before you come across a particular label, try to say the word to yourself, then look at the label and see if you got it right.

Stage 2: when you feel ready, remove the labels and try to remember the words each time you see the place where they used to be.

Papers in a hat

V6

Crosswords

V7

What is it good for?

This is a classic method for memorising short items. People like it because you can test yourself at random on a wide range of items and get immediate feedback. It can be used ...

* to learn new words;

* to learn short sentences in the foreign language (▶ Possible follow-up to **[V3]** *Made-up sentences*);

* in languages where verbs have conjugations: to learn the forms of different verbs in a particular tense;

* in languages that use cases: to learn declensions.

How to proceed

1   Prepare the items:

* *Single words or short sentences:* write the word or short sentence to be learnt on one side and the English translation on the other.

* *Verb conjugations, noun declensions, etc:* write the English translation of the word on one side, and the full list of forms on the other.

2   Fold the papers into four, put them in a hat (a box or a bag will do just as well). Draw out one paper at a time and try to provide the required item in the foreign language.

3   If your answer is correct, remove the paper from the hat. If it isn't, put the paper back in. Carry on until there are no papers left in the hat.

How to assess progress

Simply repeat the same task on successive days until you get all the items on the first attempt. You may wish to hold on to the papers for revision purposes.

What is it good for?

This is a good technique for memorising new words, especially if spelling is a problem for you. If you use short sentences in the foreign language as clues (instead of just an English translation of the word), you will also be practising your writing, and you will be learning the words in context, which is a better way of learning them.

How to proceed

1   Create a 'master grid' that includes all the words that you want to learn. Then make a copy of the grid with the letters left blank.

2   For the clues, write up simple sentences that include the words, leaving blanks where the words in question would have been. Alternatively, write the definitions for the words in the target language. Try not to resort to simple translations of the words into English!

3   If you have the chance, you may get a competent speaker to check through the clues that you have written.

4   Put the crossword away and try to do it a few days later when you have forgotten what the words were, or try it out on somebody else.

How to assess progress

Like in any other crossword: if it all fits in, it means that you got it right! But what really matters is that you end up able to use the words. So try to re-use them in real communication at the earliest opportunity (▶ **[V9]** *Recycling*).

![KEY TERMS]

Conjugation = the set of variations in forms that verbs in some languages use to show their subject, e.g. Bosnian/Croatian/Serbian *volim* (I love), *voliš* (you love), etc or French: *j'aime, tu aimes,* etc.

Declension = the set of variations in forms shown by nouns and adjectives in some languages. Forms usually vary according to number (singular/plural), e.g. Spanish: casa > casas and **case** (the word's role in the sentence), e.g. Bosnian/Croatian/Serbian *televizija* (television: subject), *televiziju* (television: object).

V8 | Anagrams

V8
V9

What is it good for?

This is a good technique for memorising new words, especially if spelling is a problem for you.

How to proceed

1 Take a simple word list (no more than 5–10 words) based on a common topic, and write the words in large capital letters on a piece of paper.

2 With a pair of scissors, cut out the words into individual letters and mix them all up on a table.

3 Put the letters into the right order again to reconstruct the original list.

4 A good follow-up is to try to make up different words using as many of the original letters as possible (as you do in a game of *Scrabble*). Use the dictionary if you have doubts about a particular word.

How to assess progress

• Keep the pieces of paper and repeat the exercise at a later date.

• Try to re-use the words in real communication at the earliest opportunity (▶ **[V9]** *Recycling*).

V9 | Recycling

What is it good for?

The more you use a word, the more likely you are to remember it. You should always try to re-use what you just learnt in real communication. This doesn't only apply to single words, but to everything you may learn, from voice intonation on a particular phrase to the use of a given tense. Here are just a few tips.

How to proceed

If you are working on your own:

• Write short passages using the language that you just learnt (see below for ways in which to monitor your progress).

• Carry out imaginary conversations based on the topic you just covered (▶ **[S6]** *Imaginary chats*).

If you have a partner:

• Try to recycle certain items when you are simply talking or writing to each other. Some learners have a 'word of the week' that they try to place at every opportunity during that period, but it could also be a 'tense of the week', or a skill such as 'telling the time' (you would spend the week grabbing every opportunity to tell the time in the foreign language). It is very effective and your temporary 'obsession' can be great fun for both partners.

How to assess progress

Practice in itself is useful, even if you can't always obtain feedback. Some learning is taking place every time you try to use the language, even if you make mistakes.

Feedback on written practice

• If you have access to a competent speaker (native speaker, teacher, or another learner), don't hesitate to ask them to look through what you have written.

• If you are entirely on your own, you can still assess your performance by setting the work aside for a while and looking at it again at a later date. You will spot a few mistakes by yourself, and may realise you've made progress since then!

Feedback on spoken practice

• Other speakers will probably only give you explicit feedback if you ask them to. Facial expression (a barely perceptible smile) can also indicate that you have said something slightly odd. Ask them to tell you what made them smile!

• One way to evaluate your performance without ruining the conversation is to record it and go through it together afterwards. You could even transcribe your own words and analyse the mistakes (▶ **[G5]** *Self-transcript*).

chapter

7

Grammar

What does learning grammar involve?

What is grammar?

If vocabulary is the bricks of the language, grammar is the mortar that holds the bricks together – in other words, it shows the relationships between different concepts. Traditionally, grammar is divided into two areas, morphology and syntax:

- **Morphology** shows how words change internally: e.g. *come* can change to *coming, comes* or *came*.

- **Syntax** shows how different words can be chained together: e.g. *she'll be coming round the mountain when she comes*.

Also, there are some aspects of language that can be seen as mid-way between grammar and vocabulary, such as:

- **Particles:** little grammar words, e.g. *the, a, of, when*.

- Principles of **word-formation:** how new words are made from old, e.g. *light > lighten, white > whiten*.

How languages use grammar

Though most languages use all four aspects of grammar, the importance of each – and hence the task you face as a learner – can vary from language to language.

Some languages, like Chinese or (to a certain extent) English, rely on syntax and particles. Words have few if any 'endings', but word-order is crucial (e.g. *The man bit the dog* is a different real-world event from *The dog bit the man*). Learning grammar here is mainly a matter of learning basic sentence patterns – by repeating cassette dialogues, for example.

Other languages rely on morphology. Here, words can take very complex sets of forms depending on whether they are the subject or object of the sentence, singular or plural, etc. Word-order, however, is usually less strict. These languages fall into two types:

- **Agglutinative** languages (like Hungarian, Turkish or Japanese) use long chains of morphemes after the main word (a morpheme is a set of letters/sounds, such as *-ing* or *-s* in English, that alters a word's grammar). Each morpheme has one and the same meaning. In Hungarian, for example, *-k* makes words plural, and *-nak* means *to/for*; so *to the professors* is *a professzoroknak* and *for the televisions* is *a televízióknak*. This results in words that look mind-bogglingly complex at first sight. But because the meaning of each particle is always the same, the learning load isn't actually that bad.

- With **synthetic** languages there isn't a clear one-to-one link between form and meaning. The Russian for *cards*, for instance, is *karty* but for *windows* is *okna*; or the Welsh word *mam* (*mother*) can change to *fam* for a number of completely unrelated reasons. This type of grammar is the hardest to master in the beginning, especially if you don't like learning 'tables' (lists of forms). The thing to remember here is not to let these complexities put you off communicating. Even with ropey grammar, your message will get across; native speakers will usually be very forgiving of your mistakes, and as long as you're practising, you're improving.

With many languages, the rules of word-formation are very regular (English, which takes its vocabulary from a mixture of source languages, is an exception here). In Arabic, for instance, *-aa-i-* means someone who does something, as in *kaatib* (*writer*) or *haakim* (*judge*); and *ma--a-a* means a place to do something, so *kaatib* changes to **maktaba** (*library*) and *haakim* changes to **mahkama** (*tribunal*). Spotting and using such rules can speed up your learning of both grammar and vocabulary.

Grammar learning

Let's start with the good news: in contrast to vocabulary, there's only a finite amount of grammar to learn in a language. After two or three years' study, you will almost certainly have met all the grammar a language has. The bad news, as you know, is that it can take a long while to get this finite amount of information into your head. There are almost certainly rules which you can recite perfectly at home but which fall to pieces when you're trying to make a conversation in a crowded bar. Or there are other rules (not many, thankfully!) which seem specially designed to flummox the non-native speaker – like noun gender, say (is it *le* or *la point* in French?). Fortunately, there has been a lot of research into grammar learning. Here are some tips which research studies have come up with:

- There are two ways to learn a grammar point: 'explicitly' and 'implicitly'. If you learn **explicitly**, you first study and memorise the rule or the form (from a book, say), and then you practise it. This makes you more likely to use it correctly in the long run, especially if you revise the rule or table at regular intervals. A lot of real-life practice is usually needed, however, before you can use it fluently and correctly at the same time! Explicit learning tends to suit studial learners more (▶ 'Learning style', p7). It is also better for items which have a clearly graspable meaning. And/or for items which don't seem essential or prominent, and which can be hard to just 'pick up' in conversation as a result. An example here is French verb endings (*je demande, tu demandes, il demande, nous demandons*, etc). Their meaning is clear (*-ons* always comes after *nous*), but they aren't essential (*nous demand-* gives us all the information we need).

- If you learn **implicitly**, you pick up a general idea of the rule from reading or listening (to a cassette or real speech). You then try it out in practice, and as time goes on you gradually get more accurate. This teaches you the right context for the form (e.g. the fact that English *would* and *could* are often used in polite requests); and if you're picking it up from real conversation, you'll probably soon find yourself speaking fluently. Disadvantages are that it can take a long while to become properly accurate, and you might not learn some grammar points at all because you can get by perfectly well without them. Implicit learning tends to suit experiential learners more (▶ 'Learning style', p7). Also, implicit learning is better for rules or patterns which are too vague or complex to learn by heart. An example here is the set of 'rules' which tell an experienced French speaker whether a new noun is likely to be masculine or feminine – these can only be learnt by experience.

- But to get the best results, one strategy is not enough. Learning grammar well involves three key strategies: grammar **study**, **input** from reading and listening, and **real-life practice** through speaking and writing. In which order they come depends on you – your learning style, the situation (in the country or at home), etc.

- **Controlled practice** (e.g. coursebook grammar exercises or do-it-yourself translations) can be very useful for getting an initial grip on an item. But **real-life practice**, or practice that is as close to real life as possible, is the only way to learn an item properly.

- Learning a grammar point is a gradual process. The title of a famous study of grammar learning is 'You only learn by goofing'. In other words, no matter whether now you've learnt a new item, you'll make mistakes with it at first. But by practising, noting what other people say and write, and getting feedback (from other speakers or from textbooks), you'll slowly but surely become more accurate.

- Even if you feel you know an item of grammar, you may still goof in real-life situations. There's a good psychological reason for this. Your mind can only juggle a certain amount of pieces of information at a time. If you're buying a ticket at a noisy station, say, you'll be concentrating on the vocabulary of your message, on trying to hear what the ticket seller is saying behind the glass partition, and on staying polite even though your train is going in five minutes. This is using all your mind's attention capacity, and there's simply no brain-power left to search your memory for the right case-endings. The answer here – once again – is lots of real-life practice!

- The fact that we have a limited attention capacity also means that we are more likely to goof on more complex items or longer sentences. In Japanese, say, or in many clauses in German, the verb goes at the end, which can mean having to hold it in memory for a long time. As often as not, if you want to say something like *If I see your sister Sieglinde in the brewery tomorrow* in German, by the time you get as far as saying *Wenn ich deine Schwester Sieglinde morgen in der Brauerei …*, you've probably forgotten there even was a verb (it should be *sehe*, by the way). The ability to handle these 'long-range' grammatical rules is something that only comes gradually, as your general fluency and command in the language increases. So a tip for less advanced learners is to speak in short sentences if you want to stay grammatically correct!

TECHNIQUES

The rest of this chapter gives a step-by-step description of all the techniques suggested for learning grammar.

G1 | Making a grammar drill

What is it good for?

This technique can help you solve a grammar problem – so long as there is a clear rule that you can understand, which makes it just a matter of getting extra practice. Both writing and doing the drill will be good practice.

How to proceed

1 Study a rule that is still a problem for you, using a grammar book or course notes. If you are working with a partner, you may work on a rule that is a problem to your partner instead. Make sure that you do understand the rule and that you can look up all the information needed. If something is not clear, you should check it before attempting this exercise.

2 Write ten sentences either for gap-filling or transformation exercises (cues for rephrasing sentences, replying to prompts, etc). Here are some examples from English:

   • Example 1:   Prompt: *John saw a mouse.*
                    Answer: *John saw two mice.*

   • Example 2:   Prompt: *Mary: 'Please buy some bread Peter'.*
                    Answer: *Mary asked Peter to buy some bread.*

   You can also use exercises from existing grammar books as models for your own. Try to relate your new made-up sentences to facts and interests of your own, rather than using boring, impersonal sentences like the two examples above.

3 If you are working with a partner, swap your drills and try to do each other's. Otherwise, set aside the drill and do it yourself a few days later, when you don't remember the answers any more (check with a competent speaker if you are not sure about the accuracy of your language).

How to assess progress

Just count how many answers you got right. Repeat the exercise at intervals of a few days until you make no mistakes at all. You may want to have your drill checked through by a competent speaker before using it, but this should not be necessary if you focus on rules that are relatively simple.

G2 | Self-correction

What is it good for?

By looking at the mistakes you make, you can learn to avoid them, and get to understand how the target language works. Don't worry too much if you cannot get feedback from somebody else at the moment (if you can't spot a mistake yourself, it could mean that you are just not ready to take in the rule in question anyway).

How to proceed

You can use this technique with either type of output:

• Any text written by yourself.

• Any speaking task, provided that you have recorded it on tape (▶ **[S4]** *Recording yourself*).

1 Prepare the original text (or write a transcript of the recording ▶ **[G5]** *Self-transcript*), leaving plenty of space for corrections.

2 With a coloured pen, circle any mistakes that you can see and write your corrections in the space that you left. Use as much reference material as you need (books, dictionaries, notes, etc) at this stage. You may notice that you tend to make more mistakes in speaking than in writing. This is perfectly normal.

3 If you can – but don't worry if it's not possible – get a more competent speaker (or even another learner) to check your text again, pointing out anything that you may have missed out. Make sure that you understand why the extra corrections were needed.

4 Make a list of the mistakes that you can now understand, and that you think you can avoid in future. If there are lots of corrections, just focus on the ones that are most obvious to you. Grouping them by category (i.e. 'wrong gender agreement', 'spelling', etc) will also narrow down the number of items on your list and increase your awareness of general rules.

How to assess progress

• Rewrite or record the original task a few days later and check your accuracy on the points that you listed as 'avoidable mistakes'.

• Use any of the ▶ **[V9]** *Recycling* techniques and assess your progress accordingly.

• Each time you use this technique again, count how many mistakes you made under each category ('wrong gender agreement', 'wrong particle', etc). You should see the numbers go down over a period of time.

G3

G4

G3 | Getting rid of known mistakes

What is it good for?

Sometimes we keep making the same mistake again and again. We realise that we keep doing it, but just can't get rid of the habit. Tackling them one at a time can help you eradicate those mistakes once and for all.

How to proceed

1 Make a list of your most typical mistakes. You only need to consider those mistakes that relate to rules you fully understand, but keep getting wrong when you are busy trying to communicate.

2 Rank them following a combination of these two criteria: (1) which ones do you find easiest to notice once you have made the mistake? and (2) which ones seem more 'serious' mistakes to you?

3 Take the first mistake on your list and watch out for it in every single task that you do in the target language. Set a period of time (a week or two) during which your mind will be entirely devoted to correcting that single mistake. If you are working with a partner, instruct him/her to stop you every time you make the mistake. Scan everything you write at least once for that single purpose.

4 Once you have won the battle with this particular mistake, declare war on the next one in your list for a similar period of time.

How to assess progress

You should notice that the mistake occurs less and less frequently. If you want an objective measurement, set yourself a standard speaking task (e.g. talking for exactly 3 minutes), record yourself (▶ **[S4]** *Recording yourself*) and count the number of times you made the mistake in the set duration of the task. Repeat a month later, and see if you have improved.

G4 | Teaching a rule

What is it good for?

One of the best ways to learn something is to teach it to somebody else. This is a confidence-building technique that will increase your awareness of grammar, both in the target language and in your mother tongue.

How to proceed

1 Find a 'pupil' (e.g. family member, flatmate) who is willing to learn from you.

2 Study the rule that you plan to teach (go for something simple at first). Prepare the following sections:

• An explanation of the rule.

• A few examples (see ▶ **[G7]** *Finding examples*). Try to make up a few examples that refer to your pupil's own world.

• A little exercise (or a series of exercises) in which the rule must be applied (▶ **[G1]** *Making a grammar drill*). Again, try to refer to your pupil's interests.

3 Teach it:

• Explain the rule and give examples.

• Get your pupil to make up more examples (some prompts from you may be needed).

• Give him/her the exercises and provide feedback.

How to assess progress

• After your lesson, your pupil should be able to apply the rule.

• You should feel more confident than before when applying the rule yourself.

• If, at some point, you got confused, this means that the rule may be more complicated than you thought, and that you were not ready to teach it yet. Seek more information and try again when you feel ready. In the meantime, set a less ambitious goal for your next teaching session.

G5 | Self-transcript

What is it good for?

Speech is difficult to assess because it has no visible output. But by recording and writing down everything that you said, you can focus on aspects that would otherwise be difficult to see. It is also a way of correcting your grammar without interrupting the conversation.

How to proceed

1 Make an appointment with another learner and agree on a topic for discussion or role play.

2 If necessary, prepare basic vocabulary and phrases before you start talking, but make sure you don't read out entire sentences!

3 Record your conversation with your partner on an audio-cassette, making sure that it doesn't last more than five minutes (▶ **[S4]** *Recording yourself*).

4 Working on your own, write an exact transcript of **every single** word you said (including hesitations, mistakes, false starts, etc).

How to assess progress

This technique can be used as the first step for other techniques such as the following:

▶ **[G2]** *Self-correction* (for grammar improvement and self-assessment purposes)

▶ **[S14]** *Marking your spoken performance* (for in-depth self-assessment)

▶ **[S9]** *Outspeaking your partner* (for measuring your fluency)

▶ **[S8]** *Interrupting your partner* (to improve fluency and turn-taking skills)

G6 | Chop and jumble

What is it good for?

Finding a suitable passage on which to use this technique is in itself an excellent reading exercise. Both processes involved (cutting out the text and reconstructing it) make you think very carefully about syntax and the language devices that link sentences to each other (e.g. *'however', 'finally', 'another important issue.'*, etc), while keeping an eye on the global meaning of the text.

If you apply the technique to shorter units (sentences or paragraphs), it can be a powerful means of getting to grips with the rules governing word order and agreement.

How to proceed

1 Take a text that you can understand and that has a logical structure (like a story with a beginning and an end; an argument where one point leads logically to another; a dialogue from a coursebook, a set of directions that have a logical order from a user's manual, etc).

2 Copy (or photocopy) it onto another sheet and cut it out into a few separate paragraphs or sentences (try to do it in a way that is logical and leaves some clues).

   Tip: If you have the text on disk (for example, a newspaper article from the Internet) you can insert a paragraph break each time a new 'part' begins, and then sort the paragraphs in alphabetical order (most word-processors have a 'sort' facility). This will jumble them for you.

3 If you are working with a partner, swap texts and try to re-arrange the paragraphs/sentences again as a coherent text. Otherwise, set aside the text and do it yourself a few days later, when you don't remember the original anymore.

How to assess progress

Compare the reconstructed version to the original, bearing in mind that the original order may not be the only possible one. Any discrepancies should be analysed critically to see whether they make sense (both from meaning and grammar points of view).

G7

G8

Finding examples

G7

What is it good for?

Grammar books may lead to 'tunnel vision' by offering mostly single-sentence examples out of context. This technique gives you a chance to look at the context in which language rules actually operate. Being able to recognise a language form when you come across it is also the first step towards being able to use it. Finally, examples that you have compiled yourself are more likely to stay in your memory.

How to proceed

1   For every new rule of grammar that you learn, prepare a blank sheet that you can insert in your grammar book or personal notes. It may be a good idea to keep a personal grammar log book in which you record the rules as you learn them. A ring binder will allow you to insert new pages and rearrange the material as needed.

2   Over a period after you study each new rule, look out for as many examples of this rule as you can find in the materials that you normally use for reading and listening. Try to find a minimum number of examples for each rule (say ten) and write them down on your grammar log book.

3   Use these examples for ▶ [W2] *Back translation.* They would also be suitable for other learning techniques such as ▶ [V6] *Papers in a hat,* ▶ [V9] *Recycling,* and ▶ [G8] *Learn it by heart.*

How to assess progress

Just count the examples on your list. You could also show them to somebody else and discuss how representative they are of the rule that you intended to demonstrate. You will know that the exercise has worked when you start using the rule automatically in your writing and speaking.

Learn it by heart

G8

What is it good for?

A tried and tested technique, excellent for retaining vocabulary, typical sentence structures, verb forms, etc. You will then discover that you are able to use these patterns and words automatically as they spring to your mind as ready-formed blocks whenever you need them.

How to proceed

Choose a short news flash, a poem, a song, a language coursebook dialogue (if you work with a partner), an extract from a speech, etc – any short text that looks interesting or useful. Learn it by heart and say it out loud as convincingly as you can.

How to assess progress

See how much of the text you remember a few days later and re-learn the parts that you have forgotten. You can also record yourself and improve your acting as you practise. Sooner or later, words, phrases or sentence patterns from the text will spring to your mind automatically as you speak about something else.

Seeking feedback

G9

What is it good for?

In matters of language accuracy, knowing whether or not you got it 'right' is important. Unfortunately, getting feedback is often difficult for independent learners. Here are a few ways in which to bridge the gap.

How to proceed

- Look for books that have an answer key.

- Your local resource centre may have computer software for language learning. Language CD-ROMs often give good feedback and are fun to use. Ask!

- Use existing texts as a starting point to create your own grammar exercises: see for instance ▶ **[W3]** *Creating a gapped text,* **[G6]** *Chop and jumble,* **[G7]** *Finding examples.*

- The technique of ▶ **[W2]** *Back translation* is very popular because the original text is a ready-made model. A variation is to take example sentences from a coursebook and use them for back translation (preferably in a different order from the book). The ▶ **[V6]** *Papers in a hat* technique can also be used with this type of sentences.

- Use whichever people are available at the time:

  1 Work with other learners: Do the tasks together, correct each other's work, prepare a joint list of questions that you would like to ask a teacher. Your own weaknesses might well be your partner's strengths, and vice versa.

  2 Try to find a competent speaker who can answer occasional questions and check through your work. Remember that it doesn't have to be a native speaker or a teacher of the language.

  3 If you are attending a class, use your teacher, even if your study plan covers different material from the course's syllabus (prioritise your questions if time is at a premium).

- The questionnaires shown in ▶ **[W16]** *Marking your written performance* and **[S14]** *Marking your spoken performance* are specially designed for those who do not have access to a competent speaker for feedback.

- Use your own judgement! Many of the mistakes that you make may be just due to mental overload while trying to do many things at the same time. When you pay attention and have time to check through your books and notes, you can correct these yourself (▶ **[G2]** *Self-correction,* **[G5]** *Self-transcript)*

- Redo old exercises that were given corrections when you first did them. When you are attending a course, it is a good idea to collect as much corrected material as possible for later use.

How to assess progress

Feedback in itself is the best way to assess your progress.

8 Reading

What does learning to read in a foreign language involve?

Reading has two main roles in foreign language learning: it is a skill worth knowing in its own right, and it is also a way of improving your knowledge of the language as a whole. Let us start by looking at these two roles.

Reading as a life skill

Words surround us everywhere. Basic reading ability is crucial if we are to survive even as a tourist in a foreign country ('restaurant', 'bus station', 'trespassers will be prosecuted', ...).

For some learners, to be able to read is their key foreign-language aim. A chemical engineer, for example, may want to read German reports, or a retired teacher may be brushing up her Spanish in order to read South American literature in the original. Most learners, however, want a general all-round ability in the foreign language, and reading – apart from the survival ability to read signs, timetables and labels – probably does not figure very high on their list of actual 'needs'. Yet many learners have told us that reading in the foreign language is a pleasure in itself, especially once they have reached a level where they can grasp the general gist of magazine articles, comics, etc – not least because it gives an enjoyable insight into the foreign culture.

Reading for language improvement

Foreign-language reading also helps your all-round language development: no matter how carefully you memorise and practise a grammar or vocabulary item, you don't actually 'know' it (i.e. you can't use it fluently in speaking or writing) until you've seen or heard it used in a realistic context.

And the more your all-round understanding of the language increases, the more you are able to learn **new** items directly from reading or hearing them and working out what they mean from the context – a process known as 'comprehensible input'. This is much more fun than memorising word-lists and grammar rules. And reading seems an especially effective way of getting comprehensible input because (unlike with real-life listening) you can work at your own speed. For example, you might stop at times to re-read a sentence or look up a key word in a dictionary – thus making sure that everything is comprehensible, and also paying a lot of attention to key new items (both of which help learning).

The skills of reading

So what do we actually do when we read? To begin with, reading involves two key elements: converting 'graphemes' (the marks on the page) to sound, and/or converting graphemes to meaning (either via sounds, or directly).

For the fluent reader, whether in one's own or a foreign language, reading also involves a combination of two mental processes: 'bottom-up' and 'top-down' processing. Bottom-up processing converts graphemes word by word (to be more precise, grammatical 'chunk' by grammatical 'chunk') as they come in, as when reading the German sentence:

Die Katze (> the cat) > fing (> caught) > die Maus (> the mouse).

Top-down processing involves keeping the unfolding context of the whole story in your mind, and using it to predict what is coming next. Hence it also helps you decipher words which you might have misread or which you do not know. For example, in the next sentence

Sie spielte (> she played) > mit der Maus (> with the mouse) > und (> and) > verschlang (> ??) > sie (> it) > dann (> then).

you may not know the word *verschlang*, but top-down processing would enable you to work out that it means something like *ate* (it actually means *gobbled up*).

Learning to read a foreign language

So how do we learn to read well in a foreign language? Obviously, it first depends on our all-round knowledge of the foreign language, especially vocabulary: the more words we already know in a text, the easier it is to understand.

But, as with the other three main skills (writing, listening and speaking), we learn mainly by doing. Lots of practice is essential to develop fast and efficient processing. So – read as much as you can, for fun, using texts that are pleasant and not too difficult, and keeping dictionary use to a minimum. For beginners, such texts can be harder to find, but try regularly reading dialogues and texts from previous units in your coursebook, or from easy units in another coursebook of a similar level.

But also try to vary the 'extensive' reading just mentioned with more 'intensive' reading, where you stop to work on specific language items or strategies. For example, regularly give yourself fifteen–twenty minutes of reading (no more, to avoid overload) with a dictionary and noting down new words to learn. Next day, re-read the text you read intensively the day before. This will help your general language development.

As for top-down strategies, you can help improve these by stopping every couple of sentences and mentally summarising what you have read so far. And/or by predicting what the next sentence might say, and then checking whether your prediction was right. Another exercise is **not** to use the dictionary, but to use context to try to guess the meaning of every unknown word you come across (this may involve reading a sentence or two ahead). Make a mental or pencil note of each guess, and after fifteen–twenty minutes, stop. Afterwards (or the next day), look up each word in a dictionary and see how many you got roughly right – you'll be surprised how many!

TECHNIQUES

The rest of this chapter gives a step-by-step description of all the techniques suggested for improving your reading skills.

Basic reading strategies

R1

What is it good for?

A good reader does not tackle every text in the same way. Depending on the type of text and the reason one has for reading it, different strategies should be used (e.g. you don't read a user manual like you read a poetry book). This section raises awareness on a variety of reading strategies to help you improve your reading efficiency.

How to proceed

1   Read 'What does learning to read in a foreign language involve?' (p70), focusing on what the following reading strategies entail:

- Extensive reading
- Intensive reading
- Top-down processing
- Bottom-up processing

2   Now read about the strategies described below:

- *Skimming* – looking through a text very quickly, just to find out roughly what it is about (e.g. a long newspaper article, to see if it's worth reading or not).

- *Reading for gist* – reading through a whole text in order to work out its general structure and meaning (much the same as skimming, only you don't stop as soon as you get the idea).

- *Reading for detail* – reading carefully through a whole text (e.g. your tenancy agreement).

- *Scanning* – looking through a text in order to find where one particular point is mentioned (e.g. the student handbook for your course in order to check the required length of a particular assignment).

- *Reading aloud* – this strategy is used only in special cases, such as pronunciation practice, poetry reading, or reading out for somebody else. Because reading aloud is a sound-oriented strategy, it is more difficult to process the meaning, so use it only when you need to!

3   Over the next few weeks, compile your own collection of texts to illustrate different reading strategies (▶ **[R8]** *Text collections*). Try to find at least three texts in the foreign language where you would use mostly scanning, three texts where you would use mostly skimming and three texts where you would mostly read for detail. Remember that you don't necessarily have to look for texts in which you understand every single word, or texts of a 'serious' nature (a comic strip with speech bubbles is also a text!). The example below shows how the same text may be used in different ways depending on situation:

Reading my Tenancy Agreement

1) **Skimming**: *it just came through the post, and I open the letter to see what it is (I don't have time to read it now, but I want to make sure that it has arrived safely and 'looks' OK).*

2) **Reading for detail**: *before I sign it! (I must be sure that I agree with every detail, otherwise I may have problems later.)*

3) **Scanning**: *a friend just bought me a pet, and I want to check whether the agreement allows me to keep pets in the house (I only need to check that piece of information, the rest is irrelevant at the moment).*

How to assess progress

When your text collection is complete, you should be able to look at a text and decide which reading strategy is most appropriate for your current purpose and to explain why.

R2 | Choosing a text

What is it good for?

Choosing well is important to keep you motivated. This section offers advice on how to find reading material and how to assess the level of difficulty of a text.

How to proceed

Types of reading material

- **Simplified readers** (a good idea to get you started if you are below intermediate level).

- **Learner editions** of (unsimplified) books, which include glossaries, introductions, notes, etc – using the glossary means you can read 'above your level'.

- **Authentic texts** – not only literature, newspapers and magazines, but also comics, travel guides, information leaflets, user manuals, children's books, letters, e-mail messages: anything that is entertaining and/or interesting to you personally in terms of topic and easy enough to give you a measurable sense of progress (e.g. pages per day).

  NB: Don't just read one type of text: vary it!

Sources of reading materials

- Many local libraries purchase a number of foreign newspapers. There may be a foreign-language library in your area.

- Some bookshops have a limited stock of books in the most commonly read foreign languages. In larger cities there may be shops specialising in foreign publications.

- Ask for foreign-language brochures from tourist sites/offices in Britain.

- Ask other people (other learners, former learners, teachers or native speakers) for books and magazines.

- Find a newsagent that sells foreign newspapers and buy one every week.

- Search for reading material on the Internet (▶ **[R16]** *Surfing the Net).*

- Use every opportunity to find pen pals from the target country, and correspond regularly, either by post or e-mail (▶ **[W10]** *Letters and e-mail).*

- When abroad, read everything you see around you.

- When starting on a non-Latin script, buy a newspaper and see how many characters or words you can decipher.

Checking the suitability of a book

1 Rule number one is that the text must interest you! Use the skimming technique (▶ **[R1]** *Basic reading strategies*) to check whether the general topic and approach are likely to interest you. You can also use any summaries and reviews available to you (look at the back cover).

2 If you tackle something that is too difficult for you, you risk losing motivation and giving up. To prevent this, take a good look before you choose a book: read the first page and see if the text actually engages your interest (even it you still find it difficult to understand). If you don't understand it at all, look for something else.

3 Browse through the book, reading a paragraph here and there. See what proportion of vocabulary you can understand (about 60% is probably just about enough in this quick check).

Setting reading targets

Once you have decided to read a book, set yourself a target (to read for 30 minutes every evening, or so many pages per day, or the whole book in two weeks). You may slightly change this target after the first couple of sessions when you have a better idea of the real difficulty involved, but some kind of goal will give you a sense of achievement.

Go for variety

As well as books, newspapers and magazines, look for all types of written material in the foreign language. You will find some ideas in ▶ **[R8]** *Text collections.* Look for texts that require different reading strategies, use different styles and cover different topics for different audiences. Variety is the spice of learning!

How to assess progress

Counting pages in a book (or adding texts to your text collection) is one of the most visible signs of progress.

If you feel that you are still not reading enough, go through this section again and choose a different type of text. Experiment with different reading techniques from this chapter as well.

R3

R3 | Learning a new script

What is it good for?

Most European languages, like French, Danish or Turkish, are written in the same script as English – the 'Latin' script. But when a language is written in a non-Latin script, your reading speed will slow down considerably. This makes it all the more important to (a) learn to recognise the new characters, and (b) to practise reading to build up your reading speed.

How to proceed

Non-Latin scripts can be divided into three types:

(a) Alphabetic scripts sharing some letters with English

Languages with an alphabetic writing system have symbols which represent individual sounds, which are joined together to make words. A few European alphabets share some letters with English: Greek, for example, where α, κ, I, M are pronounced more or less as in English. The risk here is of false friends: Greek υ and H, for example are both pronounced 'ee'. Even so, you can learn to write and recognise the individual letters quite fast – after a few days spent copying, reading and writing words – though fluent recognition and writing will take a lot longer. Among the other languages in this category are Russian, Serbian and Bulgarian.

(b) Alphabetic scripts sharing no letters with English

Examples here are Arabic, Thai and Korean. These scripts take a bit longer to learn, as the shapes and the way that letters join up to form words are usually very unfamiliar. Studying one letter a day, it can take as little as a month to learn to recognise and write the individual letters. But it can take much longer to stop confusing letters that resemble each other, and to recognise whole words without having to spell them out letter by letter.

(c) Ideographic scripts

Here the characters represent concepts, each one usually corresponding to a syllable. An example here is Chinese. Imagery (below) can help you learn individual characters relatively quickly, especially when you realise that complex characters are made up from a relatively small set of basic elements combined in various ways. The problem, of course, is that there is a large number of characters to learn for even basic reading proficiency. The only other major living language using an ideographic script is Japanese – which also has two alphabetic scripts, often using all three systems in any one sentence!

TIP 1
Learning the letter-shapes: keyword-images

You can memorise non-Latin alphabetic characters by making them into 'images' that remind you of the sound of a 'keyword' – e.g. the Greek letter Γ (= G) looks like a **G**allows.

With Chinese/Japanese ideographic characters, you can use the etymology (history) of the character to give you the image – for example, zi (*little*) was originally a picture of a baby with arms outstretched. With more complex characters in Chinese, as your knowledge increases you can identify the radical ('means something like … ') and phonetic ('sounds like … ') elements in the character, and use them to make a keyword-image. Zì 字 (which means 'written character'), for example, sounds like zǐ (子: *baby*), and means something protected (宀: under a *roof*): for your keyword-image, imagine a baby in a playpen in a library, scribbling a character on a book. There are books of ready-made cartoons describing the history of Chinese and Japanese characters (e.g. H. P. Tan's *Fun With Chinese Characters*: Straits Times Press, Singapore, 1980). Get hold of them!

TIP 2
Recognising words: highlighting headlines

Every two weeks, buy a copy of the same foreign newspaper. Take one page, look at all the headlines, and highlight (with a highlighter pen) all the words you recognise. Fold the page away and keep it.

TIP 3
Recognising words: jumping at print

To build up instant ('sight') word recognition, do the same task as fast as possible. Highlight all the words you think you recognise, but *don't* pause to puzzle them out. Next day, check all the words you've highlighted: how many did you really know, and how many were look-alikes?

TIP 4
Read lots

The more you practise, the better you get. So try to read at least a paragraph a day, and more as your overall command increases. Especially, re-read passages you've studied a day or two before: you won't be worrying so much about the meaning, so you can focus at getting fluent recognition.

TIP 5
Dictionary work

Foreign-script dictionaries can be daunting at first. Even with Greek or Russian, the alphabet order will be different to English. With more exotic languages, dictionaries may follow very different systems – in Arabic, for example, you look at word-roots (so *darasa*, *mudarris* and *madrasa* – *learn*, *teacher* and *school* – are together in the dictionary). Get an expert in the language to show you how to use the dictionary. For ready reference while you're looking up words, make a bookmark from white card showing the letters of the alphabet in order. Practise reading new texts with your dictionary: sooner than you think, you'll find yourself getting a rough-and-ready idea of alphabetical order, and your look-up speed will increase.

Tip 6
Handwriting

Funnily enough, it's often easier to write a foreign script than read it. Start by copying letters, words, etc from your coursebook. Pay especial attention to how different letters join together, or (in Chinese and Japanese) the order of strokes. One warning: make sure that the book is really teaching you the hand-written form, not the printed form (as you know from English, the two are very different!).

Tip 7
Write lots

Your handwriting will improve with practice, so write lots. Keep a daily diary. Write labels for things round the home, and stick them in place. Write some in small letters, and some in capitals (if your language doesn't have smalls and capitals, choose different handwriting styles), and then change over (write new labels in capitals instead of smalls, etc) after a week.

How to assess progress

With *Tip 2*, count the words you highlight on your newspaper pages. Over the months, you will see that you have highlighted more and more words: a sure sign that your reading vocabulary is increasing.

With *Tip 3*, count all the words you identified correctly. Over the months, there should be more and more. (Ignore your 'mistaken identities': they might well increase too, but that's just a sign of your growing confidence!).

R4 | Improving visual perception

What is it good for?

Poor vision is an added difficulty when you read in a foreign language. Even if your eyesight is good, you need larger, clearer script than in your mother tongue. The following tips could make you more comfortable and improve your reading performance.

How to proceed

Here the golden rule is: if there is anything you can do to make your reading more comfortable (even just a little), just do it! Don't be afraid to ask for any of the features below if they can be of any help at all.

- *Large text size*: if you have a choice, go for large-print editions. For shorter texts (up to a few pages), it may be worth making an enlarged photocopy of the original.

- *Good contrast*: if you can't choose your source, try to make a darker photocopy. Photocopying onto coloured paper may also improve contrast (yellow works best for many people, but try different colours until you find the best one for you). You can also buy transparent coloured plastic sheets that you can put on any page while you read it.

- *Distance from the text*: use a book stand to get the text closer to your eyes (it will also protect your back). If sitting on a couch, put a cushion on your lap and rest the text on it.

- *Good lighting*: sit by the window and try to use daylight whenever you can. Otherwise, use the best lighting for you (ask your doctor or optician for advice). Don't use a single bright light on your text in a dark room: light up the darker areas of the room with a softer light.

- *Paragraph layout*: sometimes you have some control over this (e.g. if you have a word-processor file of the text). Avoiding justified texts may help in certain cases – for the reason, look at the boxes below:

| **This text is justified** (i.e. both sides of the text are arranged in a straight vertical line, as a result all lines of text have the same width). This makes it difficult to distinguish one line from the next because they all look the same. The distances between the words are variable too, which makes it more difficult to follow the horizontal lines. | **This text is aligned only on the left side**. The right side is not straight. It doesn't look as neat as a justified text, but it does make reading a lot easier for people who have sight problems. This is because every line has a different length. Poor-sighted readers can use these differences to tell the lines apart from each other. |

R5

- *Using computers*: when using texts from the Internet, making revisions on a text, etc print out the text as soon as you can and work on the paper copy. If you have to use the computer, do take a moment to set all the options (colours, font size, etc) to whatever is most comfortable for you.

- *Don't' strain yourself*: stop when you feel tired (you can focus on speaking and listening for a while).

- Find any other features that may help you (double spacing, paragraph separation, a particular font, text colour, etc) and look for them whenever you can.

R5 | Extensive reading

What is it good for?

By reading extensively, you are exposed to large amounts of input. This develops fast bottom-up processing (▶ 'What does learning to read in a foreign language involve?', p70), helps top-down processing (guessing words from context) and also helps you to internalise vocabulary and grammar forms. But above all, extensive reading of material that interests you in the target language is always a rewarding experience.

How to proceed

1 Choose a long article from a magazine (several pages), or a short book (perhaps a special 'easy reader' for foreign language learners ▶ **[R2]** *Choosing a text*).

2 Read it straight through, trying to use the dictionary only for the most essential words. If you find yourself looking up several words on every page, either:

   - you need to relax: try to do more guessing and accept some loss of information; or:

   - the text may be too difficult for extensive reading at your present level: choose something easier and set this one aside for later.

3 Of the words you look up, write a list of the ones you might find useful to know. Don't write any translations on the book itself, just underline the words in pencil (if the copy is your own). Focus on getting the gist and simply enjoying the story.

How to assess progress

Look at the same article/book again a few weeks later and compare the amount that you can understand without a dictionary. If you underlined words as you first looked them up, it will be easy to compare your understanding from one time to the next.

Alternatively you might keep a count of the number of times you use your dictionary from one reading session to the next. The number should slowly go down.

R6 | Intensive reading

What is it good for?

In this technique you make a *conscious* effort to learn as much new language as possible from a text. It is a good way to increase your vocabulary in a particular area where you may have a gap. It will also make you aware of grammar on the basis of specific examples from authentic use ('What does learning to read in a foreign language involve?', p70).

You should always use this technique in combination with extensive reading, so that you don't become too obsessed with understanding every single word. A good follow-up could be ▶ **[R15]** *Asking questions about a text*.

How to proceed

Take a short text (no more than a page) on a topic that interests you, and that you can mostly understand in gist.

Work through it with a dictionary until you can understand every single word and sentence structure in it.

Other activities

1 Divide it into logical sections and write a heading for each section.

2 Translate one or two paragraphs of 'moderate' difficulty, trying to understand how the sentences are constructed, all word agreements, all tenses used, etc (make sure the resulting translation reads like proper English in the end, even if it's not very literal!)

3 Write a summary of the text in the foreign language (▶ **[W7]** *Summary writing*). Make it no longer than a quarter of the original and try to avoid using sentences in exactly the same form as they appear in the text.

4 If you can, check any points that are unclear with somebody else (another learner or a competent speaker of the target language).

How to assess progress

After your intensive reading session, write down a set of 10–20 questions based on the text. Ideally, these should cover general comprehension, factual detail, and vocabulary. Answer them in a later session. For a more challenging test, ask a competent speaker to set the questions for you.

Alternatively, you could re-translate into the target language the paragraphs that you translated into English (▶ **[W2]** *Back translation*).

R7 | Predicting words in a text

What is it good for?

This technique is particularly useful if you need to widen your vocabulary in a particular area while also practising your reading skills. This strategy also gives you access to texts that might otherwise be quite demanding for your level, because you are only focusing on certain key words.

How to proceed

1 Find a text about the topic on which you want to expand your vocabulary. If you don't have a specific topic in mind, look at the title and the first few lines to figure out what the general topic is.

2 Make a list of words that are likely to occur when talking about the topic. First try in the target language. If you don't know them in the foreign language, write them in English.

3 Read the text and tick off the words from your list that actually appear in it.

4 Make a note of any other key words that are used, which might help you understand other texts on a similar topic in future. Try to build up a list of essential words, rather than including vocabulary that you are unlikely to meet often or to find useful.

5 Double check any new words in your dictionary (▶ 'Using a dictionary', p27).

6 A few days later, find another text on a similar topic and repeat the exercise, using the same word list as starting point. Use every opportunity to try out the words and expressions that you learnt (▶ **[V9]** *Recycling*).

How to assess progress

Use any of the vocabulary learning techniques described in Chapter 6, and assess your progress accordingly. If you need a measurable result, count (from memory) how many new words and expressions related to the topic you are now able to use.

Text collections

R8

What is it good for?

The more you read, the better you do it. Because you search and choose the materials yourself, the task should also be enjoyable and interesting and you will learn more.

If, in addition, you set yourself a particular requirement when compiling the material (topic range, text type, reading strategy used, etc), you can target specific areas for improvement according to your needs.

How to proceed

If you can, it is a good idea to work with another person so that you can exchange texts, seek clarification on difficult passages and even test made-up exercises and questions on each other.

1   Find the texts and read them: here are some ways in which your collection could be built:

• *Focusing on text variety:* collect twenty texts as different as possible from each other. Use the checklist below or make your own according to the resources available:

• a restaurant menu	• a comic strip
• the lyrics of a song	• a short news story
• an informal letter from a friend	• a weather forecast
• a formal letter	• your ten favourite newspaper headlines
• a cooking recipe	• a long article about a controversial issue
• a passage from a fiction book	• a passage from a travel guide
• a text related to your specialist subject	• a story for children
• a memo (look in 'language for business' courses)	• a job advertisement
	• an arts review
	• a sports bulletin
• a user manual	• a fashion article

• *Focusing on intensive reading:* Collect ten texts suitable for intensive reading (▶ **[R6]** *Intensive reading*) and follow this up by writing five reading comprehension questions on each (▶ **[R15]** *Asking questions about a text*).

• *Focusing on different reading techniques:* Find suitable texts for ten of the techniques described in this book (either from this Chapter or from the Vocabulary, Grammar, Reading and Writing Chapters, wherever a text is used). Choose your ten techniques, find the texts and apply the relevant techniques on them.

2   Prepare a card for each text.

Depending on the focus of your collection, this could include: the topic, the type of text (science article, comic strip, etc), a short summary (40 words or so), some key vocabulary, key grammar points (if grammar is the focus), any translated passages, and/or reading comprehension questions. Design your cards so that another learner wanting to use the same texts could refer to the cards for guidance (see ▶ **[R9]** *Text reviews* for more advice).

How to assess progress

Your collection is complete when you have compiled the number of texts that you set yourself and done any related work.

If you know a competent speaker of the target language, you could seek feedback on your understanding of the texts and any written follow-up. Swapping collections (texts *and* reading cards) with another learner could also be useful.

R9 | Text reviews

What is it good for?

In order to get a sense of progress, it is a good idea to keep a record of what you read. You are also more likely to take in the content of the reading material if you look back on it to summarise and evaluate the experience. Used as part of a text collection exercise (▶ **[R8]** *Text collections*), text reviews can be powerful learning tools.

How to proceed

Prepare a card or an A4 sheet for every text you read. Below are some ideas for the most typical text types. The total length that we recommend is around 300 words, but you may decide to use a shorter or longer format. In addition to this, you may add a section on the back of the card, listing all the words and phrases that you have learnt (or want to remember) from each text.

- *For books*: state the full publication details (title, author, publisher, year of publication); explain how you came across it; describe the book in 300 words (you can use some of the questions listed in ▶ **[S1]** *Arts review* for guidance).

- *For articles from newspapers and magazines*: state the full publication details (title, author, name and date of the newspaper/magazine); describe the type of publication (how frequent? how expensive? which topics and sections covered?); imagine the profile of a typical reader (age, gender, occupation, interests). Summarise the article, and give your opinion if appropriate (300 words for this).

- *For poems and songs*: state the full publication details (title, author, name of the book/album/journal in which you found it, publisher, date of publication); explain how you came across it; write a short introduction to explain the background of the poem/song; explain why you like it or dislike it.

- *For letters, reports, memos, etc*: who are the sender and the recipient (in terms of their status and their relationship to each other)? What is the purpose of the letter/report/memo? What is the tone of the letter/report/memo? How effectively is the message conveyed?

- *For advertisements*: where was the ad published? What is the name of the product/service being advertised? What type of product/service is this? Who issued the ad? Imagine the profile of a typical buyer (age, gender, occupation, interests). What selling strategy is being used? How effective do you think it is and why?

- *For comic strips*: state the full publication details if you know them (title, author, name of the book/magazine in which you found it, publisher, date of publication); explain how you came across it; write a short introduction to explain the background (if appropriate). Who is it aimed at (age, gender, occupation, interests)? Describe it and explain why you like it/dislike it.

How to assess progress

Simply completing the cards will give you a sense of progress. Read the texts again a couple of weeks later and see how much more you can understand now. You may also try to follow this up by reporting orally to a partner (▶ **[S1]** *Arts review*).

R10 | Predicting questions in a text

What is it good for?

If you know what information to look for in a text, you are more likely to find it. This technique activates your existing knowledge to predict what questions are likely to be answered in a text. It also means that you no longer have to rely on a teacher setting reading comprehension questions for you.

How to proceed

1   Look at the text that you want to read. Look at the title or use the skimming technique (▶ **[R1]** *Basic reading techniques*) to figure out the topic.

2   On the basis of this, make up the five questions (in English or in the target language) that a text of this type is most likely to address.

   • *Example*: For a newspaper report about a football match: (1) What two teams were playing? (2) When? (3) Where? (4) Who won? (5) What are the implications of this result for each of the teams?

3   Read the text and try to answer your questions. Tick off the ones for which the text provides an answer.

4   If some of your questions are not answered in the text, cross them out.

5   Write two more questions that are particular to this text.

6   A few days later, try to answer all your questions *before* reading the text, and then check in the text.

How to assess progress

Give yourself 100% if you managed to answer all five questions. Take off 20% for every question that you had to cross out.

Try to arrive at a more or less 'universal' set of questions that would work for every text of this kind (e.g. the five questions on 'football matches' above) and try it out a few days later on a similar kind of text (e.g. another football match).

R11 | Coffee stains

What is it good for?

By hiding parts of a text, you have to develop the skill of guessing from context, which is essential for effective reading.

How to proceed

1   If you want the task to be easier, read the text once the day before (so that you remember the meaning, but not the words).

2   Make a photocopy of the text.

3   Using a dark marker, hide some parts of it at random as though it had been accidentally stained. Another system is to fold a paper into a strip and lay it vertically or diagonally on the text (use a narrow strip with your first text, and replace it with gradually wider ones as you become more confident). In this way you don't need to make a photocopy.

4   Read the text and try to guess the parts that you cannot see.

5   Check your guesses against the original once you have reached the end of the text.

How to assess progress

1   If you understood the text overall, give yourself 50%.

2   Allocate the rest of the marks equally between all the gaps that you had to figure out.

3   Then look at each gap and give yourself half marks for guessing the meaning, and full marks for filling the gap with a word or phrase that would fit the gap both in terms of meaning and grammar (even if it is not exactly the same as the one used in the original). You may need a second opinion to assess whether your suggestions are accurate when they don't match the original.

R12 — Comparing media

What is it good for?

This technique develops the skill of reading for detail. It will also develop your knowledge about current issues and the language required to discuss them. If you combine reading-based media with radio and/or television, you will also be using your listening skills for the same purpose.

How to proceed

1 Find a news item that is mentioned in two different media. For instance:

- two different newspapers from the same country;

- one newspaper from your country and one from the target country;

- one newspaper article and one news report from the television/radio (in English or in the target language).

 The Internet (▶ **[R16]** *Surfing the Net*) can be a good tool for finding related articles because many newspapers offer a 'search' facility on their websites.

2 Divide a sheet of paper into two columns and label them according to the two media chosen (e.g. Column A: English article; Column B: article in the target language).

3 First, look at the factual information reported (i.e. not analysis or opinions, just facts). Write down each fact mentioned in the relevant column. When the same fact is mentioned in both media, note the second mention opposite the first.

4 Do the same thing with any opinions or analysis given in the two media. See if you can see any reasons for the differences between the texts.

5 Finally, compare the style in which the two media tackle the information overall. Is the tone the same in both? Why could this be?

6 You may repeat the task using more than two media.

How to assess progress

After doing this task you should be able to give a report (oral or written) about the way in which the two media tackled the same information. You can use this in two ways:

- For compiling your personal collection of material on a particular issue (as preparation for project work, for instance).

- As a starting point for discussion with a partner.

If you do this type of work over a period of time, you will notice that you become more confident when discussing current issues in the target language, both in terms of command of the necessary language and background knowledge.

R13 — Highlighting

What is it good for?

When reading a long text, it is easy to lose sight of its general structure. By physically highlighting the most relevant parts on the text itself, you should begin to see the whole wood (meaning and structure) rather than every single tree (the words). Highlighting can also be used as the first stage of ▶ **[W7]** *Summary writing*.

How to proceed

1 Start with a text of moderate length (no more than one page if the print is roughly the same size as in this book). Try to use a text that makes a point rather than a simple list of facts or events.

2 Make a photocopy of the text so you can write on it.

3 Use the skimming technique (▶ **[R1]** *Basic reading strategies*) and try to figure out how many different parts the text could be divided into (say up to five parts). Draw a horizontal line under the last paragraph of each part.

4 Give each part a title (up to ten words, preferably in the target language) and write it in the margin.

5 Use a brightly-coloured highlighter pen to mark the one sentence that could best summarise each part. No more than 10% of the whole text should be highlighted in this way: you may have to select only part of a key sentence if sentences are very long.

6 Now choose another, less prominent colour and underline other ideas that are relevant to the internal structure of each part (these may be isolated words, phrases or short sentences). No more than a quarter of the text should be underlined or highlighted.

7 Draw up a diagram with the basic skeleton of the text.

- First write down the titles that you gave to the different parts (Step 4 above). Make sure you leave lots of space between the different parts and number them.

- Under each title, copy the key sentence that you highlighted for this part (Step 5 above). Use inverted commas for this.

- Finally, arrange the remaining material that you underlined for each part (Step 6 above) in a logical way (bulleted lists for instance).

How to assess progress

When you read only the parts that you have highlighted in a bright colour (Step 5), the sum of these selected sentences should make sense and reflect the general structure of the text.

Just by looking at the final skeleton (Step 7) another person should be able to imagine what the text says without looking at the text in question. Get a partner to do this, then show him/her the original text and discuss the accuracy of your outline.

| R14 |
| R15 |

R14 | Recall techniques for reading

What is it good for?

In order to be able to recall what you have just read, you need to hold the meaning of the message in your head as efficiently as possible. This forces you to organise the message in a logical way that makes sense to remember – an important strategy for general reading skills.

How to proceed

There are two ways to recall a text: all in one go, or section by section.

Technique A – All in one go

1   Read the text. If you read it only once, try to notice how it is structured (what are the main parts) while you read it. You may allow yourself to read it twice, in which case you could focus on structure and general meaning the first time, and on additional detail the second time.

2   Step 2 (recall) can be done either in writing of orally. In any case, try to say as much as you can remember and to follow the original structure of the text as closely as possible (use the target language if possible).

Technique B – Section by section

1   Read the text one paragraph at a time. For longer texts, you may read several paragraphs at a time (deciding when to stop is in itself a reading strategy, as you should normally do it when you sense that a new section is about to begin).

2   Again, you may recall each part either in writing or orally, either in English or in your mother tongue. In any case, try to say as much as you can remember from the section that you just read.

How to assess progress

Read the text again and check how much you remembered. Look at any parts that you didn't recall and try to see what may have been the problem (less important points, comprehension problems, *etc*).

R15 | Asking questions about a text

What is it good for?

Asking questions (even if you cannot always answer them accurately) makes you look at a text more closely than if you just read it for general comprehension purposes.

How to proceed

1   Choose a text that interests you and that you can roughly understand without a dictionary.

2. Read it. Here you could use different techniques, depending on your needs (▶ **[R14]** *Recall techniques for reading,* **[R6]** *Intensive reading,* **[R10]** *Predicting questions in a text*)

3   Write down a few questions about what the text says. It doesn't matter if you are not sure about all the answers at this stage.

   • *If your level is beginner/elementary:* any five questions based on the text should be enough. The questions themselves don't need to be in the target language.

   • *If your level is intermediate or above:* try to write five questions based on the general meaning; and five more questions on details. Try also to use the target language.

4   Answer the questions:

   • First try without a dictionary, then use any means available to answer the questions.

   • Try it once in the target language (for speaking/writing practice) and once in English (to avoid parroting the original text).

   • Don't worry too much if you are working alone and are not sure about all the answers.

   • If you are working with a study partner, first try to answer the questions yourself. Then compare your two sets of questions and try to answer each other's. Go through the answers together afterwards.

How to assess progress

• *If you are working alone*: count your questions and answers: give yourself one point for each question written and one point for each answer. If you wrote all the questions recommended in Step 3, you've already scored 50% of possible marks.

   You may show the text later to a competent speaker, to check your answers and clarify what you don't understand.

• *If you are working with a study partner*: use each other to fill as many gaps as you can. Give your joint performance a score, using the system explained above.

Surfing the Net

What is it good for?

The Internet is an easy way to gain access to virtually any kind of reading material that you can think of. This section will just give you a few tips to get started.

How to proceed

Useful Web sites

Here are a few sources of information that you may find of interest. No language-specific information has been included here, but it can be quickly reached using the sites below. Please note that some addresses may have changed by the time you read this book.

- **Search engines**. They allow you to enter a keyword (in the target language if you want) and tell you all the Web pages in which that word is found. Take the time to read the 'Help' section if you are a first time user. Here are two of the most widely used search engines:

  Alta Vista
  www.altavista.com

  Yahoo
  www.yahoo.com

- **Sites for foreign languages**. Many sites offer links with a range of useful web pages for language learners. The ones given below are arranged by country/language so that you can easily select your chosen language (less commonly taught languages may not be represented in all of them).

  Lingu@NET
  www.linguanet.org.uk
  This is a website for language teachers run by CILT and NCET, offering information on sources of learning materials for foreign languages. It is a good starting point for those who are new to foreign resources on the Internet.

  EuroTV
  www.eurotv.com/
  Gives up-to-date information on satellite television daily schedules for the main European channels.

  TV Schedules of the World
  www.buttle.com/tv/schedule.htm
  For channels not covered by EuroTV. This service is more comprehensive, but not as user-friendly as EuroTV.

  International Tandem Network
  www.tcd.ie/CLCS/tandem/index.htm
  This is a network of institutions who pair up their students with students from the relevant foreign country so that they can collaborate in learning each other's language (tandem learning). The site is run by Trinity College, Dublin, and registration is free.

- **Internet resources for language teachers and learners**

  www.hull.ac.uk/ctillangsite
  This extremely useful site is run by the CTI at Hull University. It is a quick way to find resources in virtually any language. Just click on 'Site Map' to find what is available at a glance, including on-line radio and TV stations, newspapers, dictionaries and grammars, language-specific search engines and bookshops, and a whole range of resources for the less commonly taught languages.

  COMFM
  www.comfm.com
  This site offers access to over 4,000 radio stations, 400 live TV channels and 2,000 webcams from around the world. You may need to download the software required (e.g. RealAudio) if it is not already installed on your computer.

  Kidon Media-Link
  http://kidon.com/media-link/
  A bit similar to COMFM (above), this site has links with newspapers, magazines, and news agencies from around the world as well as television and radio stations. Again, you may need to download the software required (e.g. RealAudio) if it is not already installed on your computer.

  Paperboy
  http://thepaperboy.com/
  Access to a comprehensive range of newspapers from around the world. It also has 'News Search Tools' that can be useful if you are looking for a particluar item or topic.

  Your Dictionary
  www2.yourdictionary.com/index.shtml
  Ths site has links with on-line dictionaries in over 200 different languages, including specialist dictionaries (in law, business, medicine, sports, etc). It also covers a long list of on-line grammars in just as many different languages (including Klingon!).

Using the Web

- **Virtual tourism** (suitable even for beginners). Using *Lingu@net* or the *World Language Pages* as a starting point for accessing tourist information, organise a virtual holiday in the foreign country (choose a particular region and look at different hotels, tourist attractions, leisure activities and transport). Get as much information as possible (including costs) and write for more. If you prefer a more relaxed approach, just browse around and try to understand the information that you find.

- **Your specialist subject**. If you are planing to study abroad, look for the Web pages of departments similar to your own in the target country. Most universities now have Web pages, and some courses even put their lecture notes on the Web (a valuable source of reading material on your specialist subject). Use search engines to find other institutions that may be of interest (professional associations, etc). You may even find the e-mail addresses of people who could answer your queries on matters of specialist terminology or factual information).

- **Foreign newspapers**. Many newspapers allow you access free of charge. You can often do searches for a particular topic within a number of past issues of the paper, which is useful for some of the techniques described in this book (▶ **[R12]** *Comparing media*, **[L13]** *Prepared listening*)

- **Hobbies and personal interests**. Use a search engine to find information about your personal interests in the target language. Use any relevant material as a basis for reading tasks. Join a discussion group in the target language related to your personal interests (you don't necessarily have to write messages yourself!).

R17 | Hybrid texts

What is it good for?

In order to work out which sentences belong to which text you need to look for clues about text topic; and then, to re-arrange them in the correct order, you need to examine any clues given either by grammar or logical meaning. This technique is quite similar to ▶ **[G6]** *Chop and jumble*, using material from two different texts.

How to proceed

1   Take two different texts of similar length. The more similar in topic and style, the more demanding the task will be. If you prefer to have a laugh, take two very different texts.

2   Chop them into bits and jumble them together as explained in Step 2 of ▶ **[G6]** *Chop and jumble*. If you want to have a bit of fun while doing useful grammar practice, try to mix the two texts in a way that makes sense grammatically, however surrealistic the meaning might be (if you are working jointly with a partner, this stage could be the main activity of the task).

3   Unless you can swap your 'hybrid' with one prepared for you by a study partner, wait a few days or weeks (until you have forgotten the original versions) before you try to reconstruct the initial texts.

How to assess progress

You can use the same assessment technique as for ▶ **[G6]** *Chop and jumble*.

If you tried to arrange your 'hybrid' in a grammatically logical sequence, you could try to imagine a crazy story in which your surrealistic 'hybrid' would make some sense (this is probably best done orally with a partner).

Timed reading

R18

What is it good for?

Reading speed is one of the signs of reading proficiency. Simply forcing yourself to look at words faster is unlikely to improve your reading skills (you must understand what you read), but you can observe your natural reading speed at regular intervals and use it to measure your progress.

How to proceed

Good reading (▶ 'What does learning to read in a foreign language involve?', p70) is a combination of top-down (context-based) and bottom-up (word-by-word) processing. This is why you should alternate between Exercise A (mostly top-down), Exercise B (top-down and bottom-up together), and Exercise C (the most natural of all) at regular intervals.

Exercises A and B

1 Take a text one or two pages long from the same type of sources that you normally use.

2 Do one of the following:

- **Exercise A**. Set a stopwatch to one minute (two if you feel insecure) and use the skimming technique (▶ **[R1]** *Basic reading strategies*) to see what the text is about. Stop when the minute is over.

- **Exercise B**. Set a stopwatch to one minute (two if you feel insecure). Start reading at the beginning of the text and continue reading at your normal speed. Don't make efforts to be faster, and do pay attention to the general meaning of what you are reading (try to ignore any words that you don't understand and read on for more clues). Stop when the minute is over.

3 See how much you could understand in one minute (use the ▶ **[R14]** *Recall techniques for reading* to assess your performance).

4 If you did Exercise B, count the total number of words that you read the time given (one or two minutes) and calculate your reading speed in words-per-minute.

Exercise C

Every time you read a book, remember to look at your watch when you start and when you finish. Then calculate your reading speed in pages per minute (it will probably be lower than 1: this is perfectly normal).

You may also keep a log of your reading sessions for a particular book:

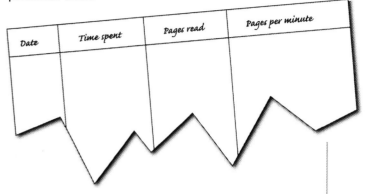

Date	Time spent	Pages read	Pages per minute

When you finish the book, look at the right-hand column and see how much your reading speed has improved through the book.

How to assess progress

If you measure your reading speed at regular intervals, you should notice a gradual improvement, provided that you get enough reading practice in the meantime.

However, some text types are simply more difficult (and hence slower to read) than others. Experiment and find out which is your slowest and which is your quickest text type. Other factors such as tiredness or a distracting environment may also affect your performance on a particular day.

chapter 9

Listening

What does learning to listen to a foreign language involve?

Listening has two main roles in foreign language learning:

- Firstly, it is a crucial skill for interacting with people: conversation would not be possible without it. And listening – not only to people, but also to foreign-language films, songs, etc – becomes an increasing source of pleasure for learners as their language ability develops.

- Secondly, listening – like reading – helps our all-round language development, both by 'fixing' items we have already memorised or studied, and by teaching new items directly through 'comprehensible input' (▶ 'Reading for language improvement', p70).

The skills of listening

Listening is the process of making sense out of sound. As with reading, it involves a combination of bottom-up and top-down processing. Before we hear a set of sounds, top-down processing (understanding the message as a whole) should tell us roughly what to expect next. For example, if you hear

The cat caught the mouse, played with it a while, and then, with a gulp, ...

I am sure you could make a good guess as to which words will follow. When the sounds actually come in, they are in a continuous stream (e.g. ... *thekadedidup*). Now bottom-up processing kicks in: we use our vocabulary and grammar knowledge along with our top-down prediction to divide up ('segment') the stream into likely word-chains (... *the cad ate it up* or ... *the cat ate it up* – but not ... *the cad edd it up*, because we don't have a past verb *edd* in our mental dictionary). Finally, top-down processing carries out quality-control tests on any word-chains that are produced: thus *cad* will either be quickly rejected as less likely than *cat*, or both possibilities will be held in memory until we have enough information to choose. Once the final selection is made, the new information is added to our top-down picture of the unfolding story.

Of course, all three processes are going on at the same time: while we are quality-checking the last bit of information, we are already segmenting the incoming speech-stream and predicting what will come next. This has two consequences. Firstly, listening to someone talking full-speed can be difficult and tiring if:

a our mental grammar-book and dictionary are so small that we have problems segmenting and fitting meanings to what we think we hear; and/or:

b we don't understand the overall context (e.g. who are they talking about?); and/or:

c the sound-stream is simply too fast for us to segment in time.

Secondly, a few sentences later, we only remember the overall picture: to avoid cluttering up our memory with useless data, the original words and grammar are soon forgotten.

Learning to listen in a foreign language

The way that the listening process works has various implications for learning how to listen in a foreign language. Firstly, in order to cope with native-speaker input for any length of time, whether from a live speaker or from the radio/TV/film-screen, we need three things:

a enough items in our mental dictionary and grammar to be able to segment and give meanings to most of what we hear;

b enough background knowledge of culture, typical behaviour, etc to make the best use of top-down processing;

c enough experience of real-time processing to segment quickly and automatically.

Ability (a) depends on our overall language knowledge. This is why beginner and elementary learners often complain that, of all the four skills (reading, listening, writing, speaking), listening is the most difficult to master, whereas intermediate and advanced learners can begin to see listening as a fun and painless way to learn. Ability (b), however, is more a question of familiarity with the culture, the topic and the speakers; and ability (c) is a question of practice.

But how can the lower-level learner get this practice if native speakers, satellite TV, etc are simply too difficult to cope with? The key tools here are audio and video players. With a cassette or video player we can listen a little, pause to think or repeat, replay again and again, and so on, until we can decipher even a difficult passage – it makes listening just like reading, in fact. By gradually listening to longer and longer passages, or by stop-start-replay listening to a passage one day and listening to it straight through the next day, we can gradually build up our skill in coping with longer and longer stretches of real speech.

Whatever our level, however, there is also a more subtle problem with real-life listening: the fact that comprehensible input isn't generally a very efficient way of building up our vocabulary and grammar base, at least in the short term. The reason for this is that we often focus so much on understanding the message that we pay no attention to the words used to convey it – and most of these words are swiftly forgotten anyway once we have extracted the ideas from them. One solution, as with reading, is to get so much input that, by being heard again and again, the new words and rules gradually become remembered. This may be tiring for lower-level learners, however, and it may be difficult for learners back home in Britain to find enough videos, audio recordings and native speakers to listen to. The other solution is, once again, intensive start-stop-replay listening. This allows learners to focus on new vocabulary or grammar by listening several times, repeating, or even taking notes.

Small wonder, therefore, that audio and video cassettes are popular with learners at all levels, and that experienced learners advise beginners never to buy a teach-yourself coursebook without the accompanying cassette!

TECHNIQUES

The rest of this chapter gives a step-by-step description of all the techniques suggested for improving your listening skills.

L1

L2

L1 | Listening for beginners

What is it good for?

This set of techniques is designed to help beginner and elementary learners get used to the sound and speed of the foreign language.

How to proceed

Try the following tips and adopt the ones that seem to work best for you.

- Expose yourself to the language as much as you can without listening actively (e.g. have the foreign radio or a course's tapes on while you do the housework). Think 'hey' every time you understand a word.

- Listen to songs in the foreign language. Learn one or two (▶ **[S7]** *Learning a song).*

- Video and television are particularly useful because you can use the pictures to figure out what is being said. Just watch and try to figure out what type of programme it is, what kind of topic/story is being discussed/shown. If you recognise the odd word, so much the better!

- Start with recordings from a coursebook that are related to the units that you have already covered. This will give you confidence before you move on to authentic (real-life) recordings.

- Use recordings that have a transcript and follow the procedure described in ▶ **[L8]** *Using a transcript.*

- Work with another learner to ease the initial pressure (▶ **[L3]** *Joint listening).*

- Get a proficient speaker to summarise the recording for you, so that you know what is going to be said beforehand (▶ **[L4]** *Tandem listening: 'Summary').*

How to assess progress

At this stage, the idea is simply to make you feel more comfortable when you listen to the foreign language. Even if you still can't understand most of what is said, you should consider that you have succeeded when these gaps in your knowledge don't matter so much anymore – once you are relaxed about your limited knowledge, you can begin to make the most of it.

L2 | Improving perception

What is it good for?

Even if your hearing is good, you need a stronger signal when listening to a foreign language (when watching a foreign film on TV, many of us need to turn up the volume above the level that we would set for a film in our mother tongue). The techniques below are simply intended to help you hear better.

How to proceed

- If you need a louder signal, don't hesitate to turn up the volume. This is quite normal when you are listening to a foreign language.

- When using audio recordings, make sure that your copies are good quality ones. Turning the volume up will not help if the recording is poor in the first place.

- Use stereo recordings if you can. It will give you a sense of space that will make it easier for your brain to filter out any background noise.

- Use headphones wherever possible. You will be able to pick up much more detail than through loudspeakers.

- Watching videos may be easier than listening to audio tapes because you can see the speakers' lip movements and body language. However the sound quality on most common domestic videotapes (VHS) is often not as good as on a decent audio tape.

- Relax! You can reduce the pressure by pausing the tape and playing again the parts that you didn't manage to hear.

- Don't struggle: stop when you feel that you had enough. Listening can be very tiring, both mentally and physically. Little and often is best.

How to assess progress

These techniques should make the message easier to hear, and therefore to understand. As your confidence increases, you will notice that actually hearing the sounds becomes less of a problem and you can focus more on what it being said.

Joint listening

L3

What is it good for?

Practising listening with another learner has many benefits: it makes you feel less anxious when you don't understand something (at least you are not the only one!). You also tend to understand more between the two of you than each of you would have managed alone (this is useful if you don't have any other means of getting feedback). It is also more fun to work with somebody else.

How to proceed

1 Find a partner who is more or less as competent as you in the foreign language (if one of you is clearly more competent than the other, ▶ **[L4]** *Tandem listening* – the next technique – may be more suitable than joint listening).

2 Choose any recording you like.

3 Listen to the recording together, using the same machine.

4 There are three possible ways to proceed:

- You may work together through a set of ready-made comprehension questions (if you are using materials from a dedicated course book).

- Each of you can prepare a set of questions that the other must try to answer (▶ **[L9]** *Asking questions about a recording*). You can also compare both sets of questions and see which points you have both seen as important and which ones have been left out (if you couldn't fully understand some parts of the recording, don't worry too much!).

- Alternatively, you may simply try to work out together as much of the meaning as possible, pausing and replaying sections of the recording as often as you need.

How to assess progress

- You should both be a source of feedback for each other.

- You may have access to an answer key (for ready-made questions) or to a transcript on which to check your hypotheses.

- However, if you only have each other, don't let this put you off. You are still getting more feedback than you would in many real-life situations (e.g. if you were on your own, trying to understand announcements in a railway station).

- Listen to the recording again by yourself a few days later and see how much you understand now.

Tandem listening

L4

What is it good for?

A native speaker can be an invaluable source of support and feedback for developing your listening skills. This is how you can make the most of your tandem partner (or of any other competent speaker who is willing to help).

How to proceed

You can use your tandem partner in the following ways:

- Ask your partner to provide a short summary of the recording for you (either in spoken or written form). You can use this summary either in order to prepare your listening or as means of feedback afterwards.

- Ask your partner to write a full transcript of the recording for you in his/her own time. You can then work on the recording by yourself and check against the transcript provided (▶ **[L8]** *Using a transcript*).

- Listen to the recording together. Ask your partner to stop the tape after each sentence and to repeat it more slowly for you. If you wish, you may also repeat it yourself afterwards in order to improve your pronunciation and intonation (you will get instant feedback from your partner).

- Listen to the recording together. Pause the tape yourself every time you need clarification about what is being said. Note down any new expressions learnt.

How to assess progress

In all the techniques described above, your tandem partner will provide you with the feedback necessary to assess your performance informally. If you prefer a numeric score …

1 Ask your partner to draw up a list of the main ideas in the recording, and to allocate a number of points to each idea according to its importance (don't look at this yourself just yet).

2 Report the content of the recording in as much detail as possible.

3 Apply the marking criteria together. How many ideas did you understand and report accurately out of the total? Calculate the relevant percentage as your mark.

L5 | Recording native speakers

What is it good for?

Conducting an interview requires good speaking and listening skills. By choosing a topic and listening to someone talk about it, you are also getting much closer to the kind of input that to which would be exposed in real life. To follow this up, you could analyse the language used and try it out yourself (▶ **[L6]** *Observing native speakers*).

How to proceed

1   Make an appointment with a native speaker to record an interview.

2   You should prepare a few questions about a topic that is relevant to you and about which the speaker is likely to know.

3   Record the interview while you conduct it (use the recording techniques described in ▶ *[S4] Recording yourself*).

4   Use the recording to learn new words and expressions in context (▶ **[L6]** *Observing native speakers*).

5   You can also use the interview for other listening techniques described in this section (e.g. ▶ **[L7]** *Writing a transcript,* **[L6]** *Observing native speakers*).

How to assess progress

•   You can check what you didn't understand with the speaker him/herself.

•   If you use the recording for other types of listening exercises, use the standard assessment techniques suggested in the relevant sections.

L6 | Observing native speakers

What is it good for?

This technique enables you to learn very much in the same way as children learn their mother tongue: through exposure to the language in use and subsequently through imitation. As you are an adult learner, you will also benefit from analysing new input consciously before attempting to copy what native speakers do.

How to proceed

1   Record a real-life conversation involving a native speaker (▶ **[L5]** *Recording native speakers)*. You may also record a TV or radio programme, provided that the speakers are not reading out from a script (i.e. don't record a news-reader). You could even take part yourself in a role play and ask the native speaker to act out his/her role as naturally as possible (▶ **[S4]** *Recording yourself,* **[S3]** *Creating a role play)*.

2   Listen to the recording and pick up a few phrases that you would never have used yourself. Work out their meanings and uses, then try to repeat them, copying the native speaker's accent and intonation.

3   You may also focus on particular conversation techniques. For instance:

•   At which point is it OK to take your turn in a conversation?

•   What phrases are used to indicate that you want to say something?

•   How do you express agreement, disagreement, respect, sarcasm, etc?

•   What is the correct intonation in each case? Use ▶ **[S10]** *Listen and repeat* to copy the speaker.

•   How loud should you be?

•   What noises do the speakers make while they are listening to another speaker? And when they are thinking while they talk? (like 'um … ' in English, 'euh … ' in French and 'eh … ' in Spanish) – copy them!

•   If you are working on a video recording, watch the body language: how do the speakers use their hands? Do they ever touch each other? Do certain intonations or phrases relate to specific facial expressions or gestures? Say the phrases yourself, copying the gestures that go with them.

4   Try to find an excuse for trying out what you have observed in your next language class or conversations with a native speaker. Experiment and see if it works!

How to assess progress

When you first try using new phrases, watch out for the native speaker's reactions when you use the new phrase (no special reaction is usually a good sign!), and check the correct meaning with him/her afterwards.

Writing a transcript

L7

What is it good for?

This exercise is particularly useful for training your ear to cope with different accents, voices and individual differences between speakers. It is also very good for your spelling (which you could get checked by a teacher or native speaker afterwards). However, most of your listening work should focus on general comprehension, i.e. use transcription only occasionally. A good follow-up could be to write comprehension questions for a partner (▶ **[L9]** *Asking questions about a recording*).

How to proceed

1   Choose an interview or any other recording that you can mostly understand (a couple of minutes at moderate speed should be long enough).

2   Write down everything you hear word by word (as in a dictation). You should include any hesitations and false starts made by speakers.

3   There may be parts that you just can't work out. Ask a classmate or a native speaker to help you (you will discover that even native speakers often cannot work out every word that is being said, so don't worry too much!), otherwise just leave blanks.

How to assess progress

The easiest thing to do is to see what percentage of the recording you managed to transcribe.

A few days later, listen to the same recording without pausing and see how much you are now able to understand straight away.

Using a transcript

L8

What is it good for?

Transcripts are useful if you really find it difficult to recognise individual words that you would recognise in writing. The golden rule is: don't use transcripts as reading texts, they are only a tool to guide your attention onto what you should be listening for. You should do this exercise with a variety of different recordings until your confidence has developed.

Of course, transcripts can also be used for feedback once you have completed a listening task, but this is not the point of the technique described here.

How to proceed

1   Find a recording that comes with a transcript (e.g. something from a coursebook, a collection of off-air material such as *Authentik, etc*).

2   First listen without looking at the transcript, trying to understand as much as you can. Do this several times, until you are sure that you wouldn't gain anything from listening to it once more.

3   Read the transcript, focusing only on the words that are familiar to you. Spot which of those would be key words for the meaning of this particular recording. Don't use your dictionary at this stage, or worry about any parts of the transcript that you can't understand.

4   Now listen to the recording while you read the transcript, focusing only on recognising the key words as they are spoken.

5   Repeat the exercise, this time without reading the transcript while you listen.

6   Forget the recording for a few days, and then try to listen to it without using the transcript at all. If you still have problems, repeat the whole procedure again.

How to assess progress

Repeat Step 6 (above) until you feel fully confident with this particular recording. You will have succeeded when you can hear all the key words without looking at the transcript. You must never struggle trying to understand every single word.

If you work in this way through the early stages of your learning, you will eventually see your confidence increase and will begin to understand more and more without having to look at the transcripts every time.

L9

Asking questions about a recording

L9

What is it good for?

Asking questions (even if you cannot always answer them accurately) helps you spot in which parts of a recording the main points are mentioned, which is an essential listening skill. If you are working with somebody else, you may also find that, after doing this exercise together, you can answer more questions than before.

How to proceed

1 Choose a recording where you can roughly understand the main idea (news items from satellite TV are a popular choice at intermediate level and above, but recorded dialogues from a course package could be used at beginners' level).

2 Listen to it several times and write down a few questions about what is being said. It doesn't matter if you are not sure about all the answers. Locating the information within the flow of speech is in itself an important skill.

- *If your level is beginner/elementary:* any five questions based on a short recording (a couple of minutes) should be enough. The questions themselves don't need to be in the target language.

- *If your level is intermediate or above*: try to write five questions based on the general meaning; and five more on details. Your recording can also be a bit longer (up to ten minutes) and you should try to use the target language.

3 Answer the questions in the same language as you used for writing them:

- *If you are working alone:* try to answer the questions yourself. Don't worry if you still have gaps.

- *If you are working with a study partner:* first try to answer the questions yourself. Then compare your two sets of questions and try to answer each other's. Go through the answers together afterwards.

- *If you are working with a native (or competent) speaker:* first try to answer the questions yourself, then go through the answers with your partner, who can then ask you further questions and explain what you could not understand.

How to assess progress

- *If you are working alone:* count your questions and answers. Give yourself one point for each question written and one point for each answer. If you wrote all the questions recommended you have already scored 50%.

If you can't get other feedback than your own, don't worry. You won't always be told 'the right answer' when you use the language in real life! Finding what questions to ask is an achievement in itself.

- *If you are working with a study partner:* use each other to fill as many gaps as you can. Give your joint performance a score, using the system explained above.

- *If you are working with a native (or competent) speaker:* first give your performance a score, using the system explained above. Then ask your partner to check your answers and clarify what you don't understand.

L10 ▎ **Extensive listening**

What is it good for?

Listening to longer recordings (watching films, for instance) can be a rewarding experience. You can relax and focus on the general meaning rather than struggling to catch every detail. One section may help you understand the previous one, and you have more time to get used to the speakers' accents. Here, the golden rule is to keep going as long as you manage to figure out (even roughly) what the main ideas are. If you are the type of learner who feels lost without a dictionary, this may be a difficult exercise at first, but stick with it for a while and the experience should be 'liberating' once you get used to it.

How to proceed

1   Find a recording that is longer than the ones normally used for listening comprehension exercises. You may use a feature film, an entire radio or television programme, a radio play, a spoken book for the blind, or just listen to a real-life conversation with native speakers. For this exercise it doesn't matter if you don't have the input recorded on tape. The main conditions are that it must be something that interests you and that is not completely impossible to understand.

2   Just listen to it (without stopping the tape if it is a recording). Don't take notes or use your dictionary.

3   Focus on the gist of what is being said and don't worry about details. The more you listen, the more you will understand.

How to assess progress

The main point of extensive listening is general comprehension and personal enjoyment. Therefore we shall not provide a set of marking criteria for this exercise. After a few sessions you will notice that you feel more and more comfortable with this type of work.

L11 ▎ **Predicting words in a recording**

What is it good for?

This technique is particularly useful if you need to widen your vocabulary in a particular area while also practising your listening skills. This strategy also gives you access to recordings that might otherwise be quite demanding for your level, because you are only focusing on certain key words.

How to proceed

1   Find a recording about the topic on which you want to expand your vocabulary. If you don't have a specific topic in mind, listen to the beginning of your chosen recording – just enough to figure out what the general topic is. Stop the tape as soon as you get the idea.

2   Make a list of words that are likely to occur when talking about that topic. First try in the target language. If you don't know them in the foreign language, write them in English.

3   Listen to the tape and tick off the words from your list that the speakers actually use in the recording.

4   Make a note of any other key words that they use, which might help you understand other recordings on a similar topic in future. Try to build up a list of 'core' (essential) words, rather than including incidental vocabulary.

5   Check any new 'core' words in your dictionary, to make sure that you get the spelling and meaning right (▶ 'Using a dictionary', p27).

6   A few days later, find a recording on a similar topic and repeat the exercise, using the same word list as starting point. Use every opportunity to try out the words and expressions that you have learnt (▶ **[V9]** *Recycling*).

How to assess progress

Use any of the vocabulary learning techniques described in Chapter 6, and assess your progress accordingly. If you need a measurable result, count (from memory) how many new words and expressions related to the topic you are now able to use.

L12 | Note-taking

What is it good for?

Note-taking is an essential skill if you are planning to attend lectures in the foreign country. Even if this is not your case, the task requires a number of skills that are important in any listening process: locating information within the speech flow, deciding what is relevant and what is not, working out how the ideas relate to each other and how the whole talk is structured. In addition, if you are taking notes or writing a summary in the target language, you will also be practising your writing skills.

How to proceed

1   First choose your recording:

*   If you are preparing for a study period in the foreign country, you should ideally look for recordings related to your specialist subject.

*   Otherwise any recording will do, provided that it does not involve too many speakers talking at the same time (a five-minute interview with one or two speakers should be fine), and that the content is interesting enough to include a number of related ideas, preferably presented with some kind of (even basic) structure.

*   A typical lecture may last up to one hour, but for this exercise, anything between five and fifteen minutes is fine.

*   If you have a real-life opportunity, don't waste it, even if the topic is not directly related to your subject: go to the lecture and take a cassette recorder with you if you can.

2   Listen while you take notes. Depending on your level and purpose, you can proceed in different ways:

*   You may vary the number of times you allow yourself to listen to the recording (we recommend a maximum of three times). Listen only once if you are in the final stages of preparing for a study period abroad or if your level is advanced.

*   Take your notes in whichever language is easiest for you: either your mother tongue or the target language. Some people even scribble their draft notes in a mixture of both languages. If you intend to write up a neat version in the target language, it is a good idea to note at least the main key words in the target language.

*   You may want to write down only the 'skeleton' of the talk, focusing mostly on gist and structure; or you may try to write down as much detail as you can possibly capture (the latter is particularly suitable if you are listening to the recording more than once). Don't lose sight of the main ideas, though.

3   You may follow up note-taking with different tasks. Try ▶ **[W7]** *Summary writing,* or ▶ **[L15]** *Recall techniques for listening,* but make sure that you don't listen again to the recording once your set number of 'runs' is over. Use only your notes and what you can remember at this stage.

How to assess progress

If you have managed to understand most of what was said and to retrieve it orally or in writing, you have achieved the goal of this task.

For more objective feedback, you can listen again to the recording, this time pausing the tape and repeating difficult sections to check your understanding. If you can, you may also check your understanding with another learner or a more competent speaker of the target language.

Prepared listening

L13

What is it good for?

Speech is much easier to understand if you know what to expect. If you know what topic is going to be discussed in a listening session (a lecture, a radio broadcast, *etc*), you can prepare your listening by finding out more about the topic itself, and of course learning some basic vocabulary related to the topic. This is common practice for professional interpreters before attending conferences on specialised topics.

How to proceed

The following tips are not in any particular order. Use whatever you can in your present situation:

- Before you watch a film in the foreign language, try to watch it dubbed or subtitled in your mother tongue. Failing that, look for a film review and read it beforehand.

- If you are going to a play, get hold of the book (in the target language or in translation) and read it before you go. You will understand it a lot better.

- Learn as much as you can about the topic itself. Find books, articles, etc in your mother tongue so that you are familiar with basic facts/concepts related to the topic.

- Try to get hold of reading material in the target language. This will provide you with the basic terminology required. If you are preparing for a course or a conference, try to get hold of student handbooks, lecture notes, abstracts, etc beforehand. The Internet can also be useful (▶ **[R16]** *Surfing the Net*).

- For current affairs, read the newspapers, both in your mother tongue and in the target language (e.g. if you are preparing for a test where the listening passages are taken from the media). You can find on-line current issues of many foreign newspapers on the Internet, and even search for articles on a particular story.

- Prepare a list of useful vocabulary and look up the words you don't know in a dictionary (▶ 'Using a dictionary', p27). Learn them if you have to.

- Write up a basic introduction to the subject (say 200 words) as if you were presenting it to non-specialists (or imagine that you are writing for an intelligent twelve-year-old). Keep your language as simple as possible, but do look up any essential key words that you absolutely need.

- Arrange to have a conversation with somebody else about the topic. Any gaps in your knowledge will become apparent as you talk.

How to assess progress

You will never be able to predict exactly all the words that you are going to need, and it may prove difficult to find the foreign equivalents to all the English terms that you have identified as key words. Your self-assessment will come from seeing how much you understand of the listening task itself.

L14

Unfamiliar accents

L14

What is it good for?

This set of techniques will help you become accustomed to new accents. This can be particularly useful if you are planning to travel to a region in which people speak with a different accent from those to which you are used.

How to proceed

1   Get hold of a recording involving speakers with the accent in question. If you know some native speakers from that region, you could ask them to allow you to record a few minutes of their speech (▶ **[L5]** *Recording native speakers*).

2   Work out the actual words that are spoken.

   - If you find the accent difficult, but not impossible to understand, you can try to write a transcript yourself (▶ **[L7]** *Writing a transcript*). There may be some gaps that you need to fill later, whenever you can get extra help.

   - If the accent makes it virtually impossible to understand, try to find recordings that already come with a transcript.

   - Alternatively, you can ask a competent speaker to write down the transcript for you.

   - If you have a tandem partner, you can ask him/her to repeat the sentences that you cannot understand, using an accent that is more familiar to you.

3   Using your transcript, observe the differences between this accent and the one(s) you know. It may be worth underlining the most striking phrases and words. Sometimes the intonation – rather than pronunciation – will make all the difference. Could you list the most typical features of this accent?

4   Select a few typical examples from your recording and repeat them, trying to copy the speaker. If you are working with a native speaker, do it both together (it should be fun!).

5   Once you are familiar with the basic rules, listen to the recording again without looking at the transcript. You should be able to understand it better than the first time.

6   In a later session, try to find a different recording of a speaker with a similar accent and repeat the exercise, or – if it's a long recording – just listen to it (▶ **[L10]** *Extensive listening*).

How to assess progress

Here are the signs that will tell you that you are making progress:

- Being able to recognise the accent when you next hear it.

- Being able to transcribe the recording (or even just part of it).

- Being able to understand other speakers with the same accent (or even just part of what they say).

- Being able to copy the accent yourself. Don't expect to sound native, just try to get another learner or a native speaker to figure out which accent you are trying to copy.

L15

Recall techniques for listening

What is it good for?

These techniques consist of repeating what you just heard, either orally or in writing. Memory has proved to be an important factor in listening comprehension. Retaining information in your memory helps you figure out the logical links between the ideas and achieve better understanding. Recalling single words helps improve your word-recognition skills and your ability to remember these words later on.

In addition, your spoken/written output will also provide practice in speaking/writing skills.

How to proceed

This technique can be used with any kind of listening material.

1   You should decide beforehand how may times you will allow yourself to play the recording (we recommend a maximum of three).

2   The nature of the input will determine the main focus of your recall exercise.

- The most typical format is to listen to the whole contents in order to write a summary of what was said. Once your number of 'runs' is over, write your summary in the target language (▶ **[W7]** *Summary writing*).

- At lower levels, you could just summarise the recording orally (mentally if you are working alone). You could even do this in English if all you want to practice is listening comprehension.

- If the recording is still too difficult for your present level, you may just focus on the most salient words (i.e. words that seem important or memorable). After listening, try to list as many words as you can. You may wish to check any new words in a dictionary (▶ 'Using a dictionary', p27).

- You could also try to remember only one or two full sentences, exactly as they were said in the recording (this works best if you are using a film, soap opera or any passage where people are talking spontaneously). Try to repeat them exactly as they were said, using the same accent and intonation.

How to assess progress

If the recording has a transcript, use it to check how much you understood.

If not, play the recording again , this time using 'pause' and 'rewind', consulting your dictionary, and using any means at your disposal to understand as much as possible. If you are working with somebody else, work through the recording together. Compare your initial recall against the information obtained after intensive study.

Repeat the exercise at regular intervals with similar recordings and compare your performance (bear in mind that progress may not be so obvious if you use recordings that are more difficult than the early ones).

L16 Using satellite TV

What is it good for?

If you have access to foreign television programmes, this section gives you a few ideas to make the most of this medium. You can use these techniques when you just feel like watching foreign TV without any specific goal in mind.

How to proceed

All the listening techniques presented in this section could be used with a satellite TV programme as a basis. ▶ **[L10]** *Extensive listening* is particularly suited to this medium.

The following tips are specific to particular types of programmes. Unless you just want to do extensive listening, it is always a good idea to make a video recording of the programmes you intend to use. Many of the tasks below can only be done if the programme is on tape.

- **News broadcasts:** write down a list of news items (with their headlines) in the same order as they appear. Compare the styles of different broadcasts from the foreign country and your own (length, structure, general tone, *etc*).

  You may also choose a particular story and try to answer the questions (don't worry too much if you can't answer them all):

1	When did it happen?
2	Where?
3	Who was involved?
4	What exactly happened?
5	Why did it happen?

- **Soap operas and feature films:** watch the different characters and work out who is who (this can normally be done using just the first fifteen minutes of a feature film, but it could take you several episodes if you are using a soap opera). Draw a diagram showing any existing relationships (this may include family trees, but also friends, enemies, neighbours, bosses, *etc*). Stop the tape at the end of a sequence and guess what will happen next, justifying your hypothesis. If you are working with somebody else, make a bet if you disagree!

- **Game shows:** all game shows begin with an introduction of the contestants. Write down their details (you can tackle this task even with little command of the language). If you are working with somebody else, describe the contestants both physically and psychologically (make up what you don't know!). With quizzes you can try to pause the tape and try to answer the questions yourself (although questions are often culture-specific). If you like speculation, guess which contestant is likely to win, and explain why you believe so. Imagine

aspects of their lives that are not actually mentioned.

- **TV commercials:** try to answer the following questions:

1	What is the name of the product being advertised?
2	What product is it?
3	What type of buyer is the commercial aimed at?
4	What is the selling point made in the commercial?

  If there is a spoken message, try to repeat it exactly as it is spoken in the commercial. Have a laugh!

- **Weather forecast:** if you are a beginner, just try to recognise as many weather-related words as possible. You can also try to recognise the names of as many regions as possible. At higher levels, you can do one of three things:

  1 Watch the picture with the sound turned right down and try to give the weather forecast in the foreign language yourself using the symbols on the map as cues.

  2 Listen to the sound without looking at the picture and try to figure out what the weather is like in different regions of the country.

  3 Imagine that you are planning a day out in a particular region, and try to understand the weather forecast for that region.

How to assess progress

These techniques simply aim to give some focus to your viewing. Just enjoy listening to authentic input and managing to understand some of it.

For more specific assessment techniques, see the relevant sections at the end of each of the techniques described in this chapter.

chapter **10** Writing

What does writing in a foreign language involve?

Learning to write a foreign language is a key priority for some learners: businesspeople, secretaries, or students studying in the foreign country, for instance. Other learners – holidaymakers, for instance – may well see foreign language writing as a fairly low priority. Our own research shows, however, that experienced foreign-language learners, whatever their needs, tend to find writing useful and enjoyable. This is because writing is not only a life skill, which some learners might need and others might not. It is also a useful means of recording and practising the grammar and vocabulary of a language – by means of vocabulary notebooks, grammar exercises, translations, etc.

The skills of writing

So what does foreign-language writing involve? Like other language skills, it is really a cluster of different sub-skills, some of which you can transfer from your mother tongue (the strategy of drafting a letter in rough and then copying it out, for example), and some of which you have to learn from scratch (handling spelling rules, for example). These sub-skills can be divided into three groups: planning, writing, and revising. Let's look at them in detail.

Planning

Any message we write – be it a brief note or a 30-page company report – has to be planned. The first planning phase comes before we write, when we plan the content of our text. This plan may be very brief (a few seconds' thought before writing a note for a friend, say), or may involve extensive research (reading up for an essay, for example); it may be a plan in our head, or one written down on paper (notes, a list of key points, or a mind-map (▶ [V1] *Word map*). The second planning phase comes while we write, when we are continuously scanning over what we have just written and deciding what word, phrase or sentence to write next.

But in both planning phases, we should ideally be paying attention to different 'text levels' at once. The 'higher' levels of planning deal with what linguists call **'discourse'**: the way that sentences combine to make readable paragraphs, and paragraphs to make logical and coherent texts. As for the 'lower' levels of planning, these deal with the nuts and bolts of sentences and words: vocabulary, grammar and spelling.

Writing

Now for the writing itself. To put our plan down on paper or screen, we need to search our mental dictionary and grammar-book for the correct written form of each morpheme (▶ 'How languages use grammar', p62), word or phrase. On the one hand, the form specifies how it is spelt. And on the other, it specifies how the actual graphemes (letters or 'characters') are formed – a sub-skill that can take a long time to learn in an unfamiliar script, as any learner of Chinese can tell you! If our mental dictionary or grammar-book can't supply these forms, or if we don't trust the forms they come up with, then we can use 'physical' means: consult a paper dictionary, copy a sample target text (e.g. a model business letter), or ask a native speaker, for example.

Once we have found an acceptable item, the brain then has to instruct the hand to form a certain word-shape with the pen, or to press a certain sequence of keys.

Revising

But good writers know that the writing process is not over once the last word has been written down: there should also be a third phase, that of revision. At the very least, this involves checking what we have written, or getting someone else (a teacher, say, or a friendly native speaker) to check it for us.

Very often, it also involves one or more re-drafts: altering our first draft on the word-processor screen, for example, or writing out a scrawled hand-written first draft 'in neat'. This revision phase is particularly important for foreign-language writers, because they are simply more likely to make errors. And these may not only be low-level errors of spelling, grammar and vocabulary. In our first draft we may have focused so hard on these low-level nuts and bolts that we may have forgotten to keep an eye on our high-level discourse plan – in other words, what we have written doesn't 'hang together' very well, or doesn't convey the overall message we had intended.

Learning to write in a foreign language

As with other skills, we learn best by doing. In other words, if you need to learn the skill of writing, write! Unfortunately, writing tends not be given much attention in most foreign language coursebooks – especially the more recent ones – so you may well have to devise your own writing programme. We give some specific activity ideas in the next section, but if you need to write as a life skill, you should try to fit these into an overall programme. This programme should have some activities focusing on individual sub-skills, and others on the skill as a whole. Sub-skill activities might focus on:

- **Planning**: for example, making mind-maps (▶ **[V1]** *Word map*); or writing out ('outlining') all the headings and sub-headings of a report before we write the text (▶ **[W4]** *Linking sentences and paragraphs*).

- **Writing**: for example, writing out words instead of saying them as we learn them from a word list; or, when learning a non-Western script, copying out a rough draft of our own while focusing on good handwriting (i.e. ignoring grammar, etc).

- **Revising**: for example, checking a text we have written once to debug the spelling and grammar, and then, a day or two later, to see if it 'hangs together' on a discourse level.

Whole-skill activities, however, are just as important – if not more so. Your coursebook may ask you to do writing activities (e.g. 'Write a paragraph describing a room in your home'). If it doesn't, use the theme of the unit to suggest an activity: for instance, if the unit is about restaurants, write a description of the last meal out you had.

While doing these whole-skill writing activities, keep an imaginary reader in mind. For example, with the restaurant visit, imagine you are writing to recommend it to a friend or to a Good Food Guide (or to tell the local Public Health Inspector about it!). The reason for this is that what we write depends to a great extent on who we are writing for: the discourse structure of a letter to a friend, say is much 'looser' than a report to a Good Food Guide (with its headings, introductory paragraph, etc), and the vocabulary is much more informal.

Probably the best whole-skill activities, however, are real-life ones. Keep a weekly diary, write letters and e-mails in the foreign language (▶ **[W10]** *Letters and e-mail*). Even if you wouldn't dare to speak with people in the foreign language, the good thing about writing is that it is much less intimidating: you can take your time, stop to consult a dictionary, and so on.

TECHNIQUES

The rest of this chapter gives a step-by-step description of all the techniques suggested for improving your writing skills.

W1 | Editing a transcript

What is it good for?

When we speak, we make lots of mistakes, false starts, and hesitations. When you edit a transcript of speech to make it comply with the rules of written language, you are becoming more aware of the differences between the two modes, paying more attention to language accuracy, and in some cases finding formal equivalents for the most colloquial expressions. This is particularly beneficial if your command of the written language is not as good as your command of the spoken language.

How to proceed

1 Take a recording in which the speaker is talking spontaneously (i.e. not newsreaders, but live interviews, *etc*).

2 Transcribe it as explained in ▶ **[L7]** *Writing a transcript*. If your recording already has a transcript, check the text while you listen to the recording, to make sure that it has been transcribed accurately. The transcript must contain all the mistakes and hesitations made by the speaker.

3 Using the transcript, rewrite everything the speaker said, removing all the inaccuracies, hesitations, false starts, *etc* that are typical of spoken language. If your level is advanced, you may even use reported speech (where a statement like *'I've never been involved'* could become *Mr X claimed that he had never been involved*).

You can choose to write it up as a formal report (in which case your changes may be drastic), or to preserve the original 'flavour' of the speaker's words (in which case you will simply be 'cleaning up' the transcript). See ▶ **[W6]** *Rewriting a text* for further ideas and advice.

How to assess progress

Read your final text (aloud if you can). It should flow smoothly and 'sound' like written language. You may want to show it to somebody else for additional feedback.

W2 | Back translation

What is it good for?

This technique is a simple way to get feedback on your language accuracy when you can't rely on other people. It consists of translating a text into English and then using your translation to convert it back into the target language. If you don't write exactly the same words as the original, you will need to think whether you have made a mistake, or simply found a different way of saying the same thing. It will draw your attention to sentence structures and words that you can understand but might never have used by yourself; and also to the fact that translations can be good without always being literal.

How to proceed

1 Take a text that you can *fully* understand in the foreign language. If necessary, use the intensive reading technique so that no part of it is unclear to you (▶ **[R6]** *Intensive reading*).

2 Translate the text into English on a separate sheet. Keep your translation as close to the original as possible within the limits of correct English usage.

Alternatively, make a 'free' translation that better captures the general tone and style of the text (this will make Step 3 a more demanding task).

3 Next day, translate your English translation, back into the target language.

4 Finally, compare your translation to the original:

• Correct any mistakes that you can easily understand.

• See whether 'translation shift' has brought about any changes in meaning between the two foreign-language texts.

• Discuss versions with a partner or a competent speaker of the target language at the earliest opportunity.

How to assess progress

Just by checking your version critically against the original, you will realise a number of mistakes that you can easily correct yourself.

Occasionally you might not know whether your translation is actually correct in spite of being slightly different from the original. Ask somebody else to help you with such questions.

W3 | Creating a gapped text

W4 | Linking sentences and paragraphs

What is it good for?

Instead of relying on teachers and course books for vocabulary and grammar exercises, you can create your own gap-filling exercises using this technique, and base them on your personal interests and needs. Your own learning goals should determine what words you decide to use as gaps (see some ideas under Step 3 of the procedure below).

How to proceed

1   Choose a text that you can understand.

2. Make a photocopy of it.

3   Tippex out the words on which you want to work. Before you delete them, it is a good idea to copy these words in random order on a separate sheet.

    • **To learn new vocabulary:** simply delete all the words that are related to a particular topic in the text (e.g. if the general topic on which you are working is 'football', take an article about a football match and delete the words for *team, player, score, goal,* etc).

    • **To practice specific grammar points:** you could for instance choose a news story narrating a recent event, and delete all verbs that are in a past tense. If your problems are with gender/number agreement, you could delete all articles and adjectives. You could delete all verb endings (for work on conjugations); or just every tenth word at random (for work on syntax and sentence meaning). If you are studying a language that uses declensions, you could delete the endings of all words belonging to a particular group. If you want to learn how to relate ideas and link sentences together, delete all linking words such as *however, and, or, if, besides, finally, though ...* , and so on.

4   Leave the text and the word list aside for a few days (until you have forgotten the original version). Alternatively, you can work with a partner and swap your texts once you have created the gaps.

5   Try to fill in the gaps that you created in the text. If you want to make the task easier, use the word list as a clue (but try first without looking at it!).

How to assess progress

1   Compare your version to the original text and count the percentage of words that you got right. If you are not sure about alternative answers, discuss your answers with another learner or a competent speaker of the target language.

2   Repeat the task a couple of weeks later and see if your performance has improved.

What is it good for?

This technique will help you learn how to link ideas in a text so that it progresses smoothly using sentences and paragraphs that are clearly related to each other. Our advice is based on three different types of writing: descriptive (texts stating facts), narrative (stories) and argumentative (texts presenting logical arguments).

How to proceed

Descriptions (texts stating facts)

1   Choose a person, a place or an object to describe.

2   Make a bulleted list of facts related to that person, place, object, as in the example below. State between ten and twenty facts, in any order you like:

> • *name = Richard*
> • *studies Engineering*
> • *blue eyes*
> • *is English*
> • *hates football*
> • *reads computing magazines*

3   Write a text that includes all these facts, making as many links as you can so that it reads like continuous prose. For example:

> *'Richard, an Englishman, is a blue-eyed engineering student who hates football and reads computing magazines.'*

Narrations (stories)

1   Choose a story (it can be a personal anecdote, the plot of a film, a novel, a children story, etc.

2   List everything that happens in the story, in the form of a bulleted list (you can even do this in the present tense):

> • *Little Red Riding Hood takes basket*
> • *leaves house*
> • *goes into wood*
> • *wolf sees her*
> • *wolf asks: 'Where are you going?'*

3   Write the story, including all the events on your list, and linking them to each other in the right sequence. You will probably need to make a number of changes (depending on your target language), such as using past tenses, reported speech and so on. Refer to a grammar book if you need to. Make as many links as you can:

> Little Red Riding Hood took the basket, left the house and went into the wood. When he saw her there, the wolf asked where she was going.

Logical arguments (texts presenting an argument)

1   Find a text in which points are made in support for or against an idea.

2   List the different points that are made and write them down in the form of a bulleted list. Remove any link words such as *however, besides, secondly, finally, although, on the other hand* – as in the following example:

> *   lots of people smoke
> *   smoking = bad for you
> *   causes cancer
> *   unpleasant for non-smokers
> *   soothing for smokers
> *   smokers regard it as civil liberty
> *   non-smokers regard it as threat to health
> *   peer pressure important (some groups)
> *   not easy to give up
> *   part of the economy depends on it
> *   hospitals would save money if fewer people smoked
> *   young people must be prevented from taking up smoking
> *   smokers must be helped to give up
> *   publicity campaigns in all media
> *   higher taxes on tobacco don't do anything
> *   alternatives (sports, etc) must be offered

3   Now rearrange the ideas on your paper in such a way that the links between them can be seen. In other words, turn your bulletted list into a proper outline:

> ### Smoking is bad for you, BUT STILL lots of people smoke.
>
> Arguments against:
> *   *smoking causes cancer*
> *   *it is unpleasant for non-smokers*
> *   *non-smokers regard it as a threat to their health*
> *   *hospitals would save money if fewer people smoked*
>
> On the other hand:
> *   *not easy to give up*
>   - *it is soothing for smokers*
>   - *peer pressure important in some groups*
> *   *smokers regard it as a civil liberty*
> *   *part of the economy depends on it*
>
> In conclusion:
> *   *Goals:*
>   - *smokers must be helped to give up*
>   - *young people must be prevented from taking up smoking*
> *   *Obstacles:*
>   - *we know that higher taxes on tobacco don't do anything*
> *   *Some alternative solutions:*
>   - *publicity campaigns in all media*
>   - *alternatives (sports, etc) must be offered*

4   Using only your outline, write a summary of the text in continuous prose (i.e. no headings or lists of points, but full paragraphs). It should include all the ideas listed, and use actual words to express all the links that are shown on your outline.

How to assess progress

Read your text aloud and listen to yourself (▶ **[S12]** *Reading aloud*). Sentences must flow naturally. If something does not 'sound' right, you probably need to make some changes. If you can, let someone else read it and see if they understand. If your partner had problems or found your prose clumsy in certain parts of the text, try to improve those parts.

W5

W6

W5 | Paragraph expansion

What is it good for?

Using more words to write the same thing is one simple way of stretching yourself a bit further when you feel that your writing skills are reaching a threshold.

How to proceed

1 Take a text that you have written earlier (on any topic) and count the words in it. Try to alternate between descriptions, stories and argumentative texts (as explained in ▶ **[W4]** *Linking sentences and paragraphs*).

2 Rewrite the text, doubling its length. The original structure should be preserved, so that the proportion of text related to each idea remains roughly the same within the final text.

How to assess progress

See assessment techniques in ▶ **[W16]** *Marking your written performance*.

W6 | Rewriting a text

What is it good for?

This technique can be used for many purposes. Generally, when you change the target audience of a text (e.g. from tabloid readers to school-children) or its medium (e.g. from newspaper to radio) you have to change the register that you use (formal, informal, technical, colloquial, academic, *etc*). This exercise makes you more aware of register, but can also be used for practising specific areas of grammar and vocabulary.

How to proceed

1 Find a text that is clearly written with a specific audience in mind. It can be a description, a story or an argument on a particular issue. Alternatively, you can write your own (look at the three boxes on the next page for some ideas). Half a page to one page should be enough.

2 Now choose a completely different audience, medium and/or style from boxes A, B and C below, and write a new text (half a page to one page) about the same topic. Try to give the same information and follow the same basic structure as in the original text.

W7

W7 | **Summary writing**

Box A
Audiences

- *your boss*
- *your partner*
- *your best friend*
- *a six-year old*
- *a customer that you want to persuade*
- *your worst enemy*
- *a colleague*
- *a group of teenagers*
- *a board of technical experts*
- *a gay and lesbian association*
- *union reps*
- *students (of arts/engineering/ business/ medicine, etc)*
- *social workers*
- *businesspeople*
- *fashion victims*
- *train spotters ...*

Box B
Media

- *formal letter*
- *informal letter*
- *love letter*
- *e-mail message*
- *report*
- *tabloid/broadsheet newspaper article*
- *script for radio (or TV) programme*
- *script for answerphone message*
- *arts review*
- *advertisement*
- *poem/song lyrics*
- *technical/academic paper ...*

Box C
Styles

- *humorous*
- *professional*
- *critical*
- *enthusiastic*
- *politically biased (right or left)*
- *detached*
- *no-nonsense and to-the-point*
- *pretentious*
- *diplomatic*
- *un-diplomatic*
- *politically correct*
- *provocative ...*
- *sarcastic*

How to assess progress

Get somebody else to read your own text(s). From the language alone, your reader must be able to figure out who the text was written for, in which medium, and for which (imaginary) purpose. You may get a few smiles if the two audiences are very different from each other.

See also assessment techniques in ▶ **[W16]** *Marking your written performance.*

What is it good for?

Summary writing involves both reading and writing skills. At the reading stage, you need to work out the general structure of the text and decide what information is most important and which details can be left out. At the writing stage, you must find your own words in order to retrieve the same information using fewer words than the original.

How to proceed

1 First read the text, work out its general structure and extract the main ideas using the technique described in ▶ **[R13]** *Highlighting* – Steps 1 to 6 only.

2 Prepare a text outline on a separate sheet (▶ **[W4]** *Linking sentences and paragraphs*). Avoid copying out whole phrases from the text and arrange the ideas on your paper in such a way that the logical links between them can be seen.

3 Using only your outline, write a summary of the text in continuous prose (i.e. no headings or lists of points, but full paragraphs). It should include all the ideas listed, and these should be well linked together (▶ **[W4]** *Linking sentences and paragraphs*). Set yourself a word limit (e.g. a quarter of the original text length).

How to assess progress

- Rewrite your summary until it is within the word limit.

- Check that all the points highlighted and/or listed in the outline have been mentioned and that the logical sequence is the same in both the original and the summary.

- If you can, discuss your summary with another person. You can also ask your partner to highlight the main points on a fresh photocopy of the text before looking at your summary.

- See also assessment techniques in ▶ **[W16]** *Marking your written performance.*

Tips for dyslexic learners

W8

What is it good for?

Dyslexia is often regarded as a handicap for language learning, but if you learn how to play on your strengths and make up for your weaknesses, you can learn a foreign language just like anybody else. Certain tasks could take you a bit longer than usual, but with a few specific tips your learning experience can become a manageable and enjoyable challenge.

How to proceed

Above all, play on your strengths!

- Dyslexic people are said to be better than average at communication and interpersonal skills. Show these off on role plays and other speaking tasks. Take initiative in conversations.

- In your written work, be as creative and original as you can within the task constraints. Make up for any possible mistakes by producing a text that is interesting to read.

- Find a study partner and organise a regular practice slot. Such study pairs tend to be successful because the skills of both learners complement each other, and you are more likely to enjoy this than working alone.

- Become a tandem partner yourself. Helping the person who is helping you will boost your confidence.

- Experiment with all your senses: make language learning as physical as you possibly can. In your notes, do not hesitate to use lots of different colours (verb endings in red, feminine and masculine nouns in different colours, etc). Make your own drawings, move things around physically (like the little pieces of paper described in ▶ **[G6]** *Chop and jumble*). Make up your own crosswords to learn new vocabulary (▶ **[V6]** *Crosswords*). Use your whole body: speak out (or sing!) the grammar examples instead of just reading them; record your classes (with your teacher's permission) on a cassette recorder; use the ▶ **[V6]** *Papers in a hat* technique for grammar as well as vocabulary; have fun! Experiment with all the techniques described in this book: when you find something that works for you, just keep using it.

- Experiment with different media. Some people prefer typing to writing by hand. Try using computers for reading and writing (▶ **[R16]** *Surfing the Net*). Use video and television as alternatives to printed media. Experiment creatively with ▶ **[W13]** *Songs and poems*.

- Use the language for real communication as much as you can (▶ **[W10]** *Letters and e-mail*). Find native speakers to talk to, visit the foreign country if you can. Motivation is the key to success.

Here is how to minimise some of the challenges that some dyslexic learners may experience. Note that different people may find certain areas more problematic than others:

- **Accuracy** – you may often read/write the wrong word or swap letters around, or even be unable to remember words accurately when you speak. You may also have problems understanding grammar.

  Compensate for this by playing on your strengths (see above). If you feel that you are getting nowhere with a particular exercise, don't struggle: try to change tactics. Setting a task aside for a couple of days may also help.

- **Concentration** – you may find it difficult to keep focused throughout long periods of time.

  This could be because additional constraints make language processing more tiring for you. Try changing activities every now and again; take a rest. Record your classes and listen to them again later (this may also reduce anxiety since you know that you can always catch up later). Even if you are not aware of any eyesight problems, working in better visual conditions might also improve your reading skills (▶ **[R4]** *Improving visual perception*).

- **Pace** – you may need more time than other people to complete a task.

  This is fine: allow yourself whatever time you need. It is important that you work at your own pace. Many teaching institutions give dyslexic students extra time on formally assessed tests. Find out whether this is the case where you are studying and if so, make use of your entitlement.

- **Anxiety** – stressful situations (such as being asked to speak in front of a whole class, trying to answer within a time limit, making silly mistakes on a bad day ...) may seriously affect your performance.

  Avoid such situations wherever possible. If you are attending a class, explain your problem to the teacher. Not all teachers understand the difficulties associated with dyslexia and you may need to describe the specific problems that you experience. A good teacher can easily avoid unnecessary stress in the classroom (e.g. students could be asked to answer questions in pairs rather than in front of everybody). At the same time, you should learn to cope with those situations that cannot be avoided. Basic training in relaxation techniques may help.

- **Time management** – you may find it difficult to stick to deadlines (or even to remember them!), to organise your time efficiently or do forward planning.

W9

Keep a diary and force yourself to write everything in it, including your own deadlines for the different stages of each assignment. Working with a well-organised partner will help you pick up those skills and reduce the stress.

- **Memory** – you may have trouble keeping words in short term memory or remembering words and rules that you learned before.

  Don't be afraid of repetitive work. Many dyslexic learners cite repetition as their most effective strategy. Experiment with reading aloud, making up rhymes or little tunes for yourself, read out examples onto a tape and play them back again and again. Copy them out and rearrange your lists in different possible ways. If something works for you, just keep doing it!

How to assess progress

Avoid forms of assessment which create unnecessary stress. Assessing your progress from time to time is necessary so that you know what you have achieved, but you should not feel competitive about it. Do not compare yourself to other learners; you ought to regard every new step you take as an achievement in its own right. If any of the assessment techniques proposed in this book makes you tense, drop it.

If you have one, a good study partner (or a tandem partner) can be an excellent source of friendly feedback.

W9

Writing a pastiche

What is it good for?

Copying the language of a text written in a particular style (CVs, information requests, orders, academic papers, job references, memos, minutes, etc) is a good way of becoming familiar with that style. Even if you don't really have to learn any special writing style, you may just use this technique in order to widen the range of registers in which you are able to write.

How to proceed

1 Find a text that you can use as a model for the type of text that you want to learn to write.

2 Rewrite the text, changing only a few details of factual information and leaving the rest intact. For instance, if it is a letter ordering a book, change it into a letter ordering your favourite CD. If it is somebody else's CV, change it into your own (you may need some help for this), and so on.

   With more sophisticated texts (academic papers for instance), you may not be able to re-use the original quite as closely as in the examples listed above, but you can still copy the main structure of the text and the type of language used. Make your own personal glossary of useful phrases.

How to assess progress

The pastiche must read very much like the original text. You may ask a competent speaker to check your new text. If it is a letter, send it off and see whether it achieves the desired result.

W10 | Letters and e-mail

What is it good for?

Communication is what language is all about. By using the target language in order to exchange real information with real people, you can experience a sense of achievement that will keep you motivated. Even when your accuracy is far from perfect, managing to get your message across is a rewarding experience.

How to proceed

Basically, don't waste a single opportunity to put your skills into practice.

- Find the address of the Tourist Board in the foreign country and ask for information on a particular region.

- If you have Internet access, find websites related to your personal interests (▶ **[R16]** *Surfing the Net*) and write for further information. Join a chat group that uses the target language.

- Find yourself a pen pal in the target country: ask a language teacher to help you make contacts, or write to a magazine in the target country and ask them to put an advert for you.

- Join the International Tandem Network and find yourself a tandem partner. The address is: *www.tcd.ie/CLCS/tandem/index.htm* (registration is free).

How to assess progress

In this type of exchange, the most important goal is to achieve communication. Therefore, you can regard the exercise as successful so long as you are getting some replies back. If you don't get a reply, try writing to somebody else: it will eventually work if you keep trying. With e-mails, you might even like to ask your friends if they will send you a corrected version of your message in their reply (indeed, we have friends abroad who do this without being asked!).

W11 | Dictation

What is it good for?

Dictation is a tried and tested method for improving spelling. It is also often used for testing listening skills, because you need to understand a sentence first in order to write it down. You can either have a person read out a text for you, or use a recording and play it yourself (▶ **[L7]** *Writing a transcript*): the task will involve slightly different skills in each case.

How to proceed

Dictation read out by another person

Because the person is reading out from a text, the text is more likely to show features typical of written language (longer and more complex sentences, little repetition, no hesitations …). The reader will probably make an effort to speak clearly for you.

1 Ask the other person to choose a text that you are likely to understand (or use a text that you chose yourself a few days earlier).

2 Get your partner to read the text three times, as follows:

- first read the whole text once, straight through;

- then one sentence at a time, allowing pauses for writing;

- end with a final run through the whole text again.

3 Check your text against the original.

Dictation played back from a recording

The advantage here is that you can do it yourself. The disadvantage is that no allowances are made for you (the words are repeated exactly in the same way every time, with no particular effort to speak clearly). The text is more likely to be natural spoken language and to contain hesitations, false starts and inaccuracies.

Follow the procedure described in ▶ **[L7]** *Writing a transcript*.

How to assess progress

When checking your text against the original, it is best to ask somebody else to double-check it for you, because we tend to overlook our own spelling mistakes.

If you have used a recording that did not come with a transcript, have your text checked by a competent speaker, or use the self-assessment criteria described in ▶ **[L7]** *Writing a transcript*.

Over time, if you do passages of a similar nature, you should see your accuracy improve.

W12 Joint writing

What is it good for?

When you write with another person, your skills and ideas add up and produce a result that none of you could have achieved alone. You can use the technique either for formal purposes (such as joint project work), or simply to have fun while practising your writing skills in the target language.

How to proceed

Every team has its own way of doing work together. Here are some typical approaches:

- **Fifty–fifty**: The work is divided in two halves. Each person writes his/her part. In this case, you should check each other's part and write comments for each other.

- **Successive revisions**: There is only one common draft that both partners revise in turns until a final version is reached (the *Revisions* tool on some word-processing software is particularly useful for this approach).

- **On-line**: Both partners work together throughout the entire process of thinking and writing. This approach is generally more suited to short pieces of writing.

- **Split skills**: The planning is done together throughout the process (possibly with each person specialising in the topic areas in which s/he feels most confident). Then one of the partners does most of the final writing. If you are not the one writing the final version, you should make sure that you do write some of the ideas yourself (in draft form) so that you also get some writing practice.

- **Combined**: Various approaches are used for different parts of the work (e.g. split skills for the research into content matter, fifty–fifty for writing up, on-line for the introduction and conclusion).

Task suggestions

- **Joint story writing**: make up a story together, taking turns to write one new episode each.

- **Working in parallel**: choose any writing task from this chapter and do it separately, then check each other's work and reach a final joint version if appropriate.

- **Joint on-line work**: choose any writing task from this chapter and do it together.

- **Joint project** (▶ **[W15]** *Written project work*)

How to assess progress

You can use the same assessment techniques as you would use for individual work (▶ **[W16]** *Marking your written performance*).

If you are working together for a formally assessed project as part of a course, you must also be aware of two basic principles in joint writing:

- Both partners are equally responsible for the final version. If there is something in the work that you disapprove of, sort it out before submission. It is poor group work etiquette to blame a partner for the weaknesses or to take all the credit for the strengths of a joint project.

- Because the assumption is that you have both contributed in equal proportions, it is up to you to ensure a fair allocation of the workload throughout the project. If it doesn't work out in the end, all you can do is choose another partner next time.

Songs and poems

W13

What is it good for?

Here the idea is to experiment with the language and to enjoy the results. By playing with the target language and exploring its possibilities, you are making it your own.

How to proceed

You may have a natural talent for making up songs and poems. In that case, just follow your inspiration!

If you are not naturally talented but still enjoy poetry and song, try some of the following:

- Use the ▶ **[G6]** *Chop and jumble* technique with the verses of a poem (or the lyrics of a song). Cut each line into a strip of paper, jumble them around and try to re-order the lines without listening to the song or reading the poem. This is one way to learn them by heart.

- If you have two songs, you can use the ▶ **[R17]** *Hybrid texts* technique and mix up the two sets of lines in the same way.

- Work in pairs: pick up a list of three words at random and try to write one poem (or new lyrics for a known tune) in which all three words are used.

- Translate an English song into the foreign language, trying to preserve the original meaning of the lyrics. If you are feeling ambitious, try to have rhymes in the same places as the original, and make sure that the natural stresses of the language match the stresses of the music (though in this case your translation may have to be less literal).

- Rewrite an English song into the foreign language with your own, completely new, lyrics. Experiment with rhyme and stress.

- Take a song in the foreign language, and change only a few key words to make it mean something else. It will be more fun if the new lyrics have a similar sound as the original (same rhymes, etc).

- Do the same with a poem in the foreign language.

- Translate a simple poem from your mother tongue into the foreign language. Try to preserve as much of the original flavour as possible. If you are feeling ambitious, pay attention to rhyme and/or rhythm as well.

- Work in pairs: decide on a topic, set a poetic form that you want to use – e.g. blank verse (easy) or a sonnet (hard!) – and write a poem together. Or each of you draft a poem separately and help each other to produce a final polished version.

How to assess progress

Read out (or sing) the final product and find out what it sounds like.

Keeping a diary

W14

What is it good for?

Keeping a diary in the foreign language is a way of relating the language that you are learning to your personal experience. You can do this at any level and use the diary as a record of your progress over a period of time.

How to proceed

Decide how often you are going to write your diary (if daily entries seem too ambitious, consider writing once or twice a week). You may want to use a dictionary and other reference materials every time, or alternate sessions in which you use them with sessions in which you rely only on your own knowledge of the language.

You can follow different approaches, or alternate between them:

- **Practice diary**: In each new entry, write about the last topic that you have been studying. This can be done from your very first session as a complete beginner. First you may only be able to say who you are, where you live and where you come from. A week later you may begin to introduce your friends and family, and a couple of months later you will be able to say what you did on your last holiday and discuss your likes and dislikes.

- **'Dear Diary'**: You may just write a personal diary in which you record your general experiences, feelings, and thoughts. The language does not have to be sophisticated or perfectly accurate.

- **Learner diary**: This is a diary in which you record your experience as a learner of the foreign language: what tasks you do, what you find most difficult, rewarding, useful, what you plan to do next, and so on. It is useful for developing vocabulary for talking about language, though elementary-level learners may find it a bit hard at first.

How to assess progress

- The most useful feedback that you can get on a diary is from yourself. Just come back to old entries some time later and use your improved proficiency to correct old mistakes and revise clumsy paragraphs.

- If you are lucky to have a close friend from the target country, send it to him/her at regular intervals. Whether you want your friend to make corrections is up to you.

- If you know a proficient speaker of the target language, you could just keep a practice diary (it is less personal than the 'dear diary' version) and have it checked regularly. The same applies to learner diaries, which are probably more appealing to your readers if these happen to be language teachers!

W15 | Written project work

What is it good for?

You may have to submit a written project in the target language as part of your course work, or at the workplace. Problem-solving and time management skills are just as important as language skills for this type of assignment. If you are working as a team, see also ▶ **[W12]** *Joint writing*.

How to proceed

The advice given here is fairly general and should apply to most subject areas:

1   Before you start, **set yourself deadlines** for completing each of the five stages below. Be strict about these deadlines, unless common sense says otherwise.

2   **Research**: First you need to know what information you are going to include in the document. Don't just use English sources at this stage: look for texts about your subject in the target language in order to familiarise yourself with the required terminology. If these are difficult to find, try searching the Internet (▶ **[R16]** *Surfing the Net*). Getting hold of a good dictionary should also be part of the research stage (▶ 'Choosing and using dictionaries' p25).

3   **Project outline**: Once you have most of the information, it is time to decide how you are going to organise it.

   •   Prepare an outline of the whole project, stating which sources to use for each part. If you can get hold of similar projects that have been successful, take a look at their structure and use them as models if appropriate.

   •   If you are working as a team, this is when you should decide who will be doing what.

   •   On the basis of the required length of the project, allocate a rough number of words for each section.

   •   Check your deadlines for the remaining steps of the project, stating by which date each part should be completed.

4   **First draft**: Try to avoid writing first in English and then translating the text into the target language: you risk coming up with sophisticated sentences that will be hard to translate later. If you must do it, imagine that you are writing for an intelligent twelve-year-old reader and keep your text as simple as possible.

It is actually easier (although more time-consuming at first) to write directly in the target language because you are using your own simple words right from the start. Keep checking the number of words in each part as you write.

5   **Revision**: Revision is essential to any writing work. Read through the text yourself and get others to read it as well (we often don't see our own mistakes). For assessed coursework, check whether you are allowed to get help from a native speaker for a few corrections. In work situations, do not hesitate to seek help from any competent speaker who is available.

6   **Final touches**: Run a spell checker through your text (if you have one in the foreign language), and then have it proof-read by another person *as well* – as you know from English writing, spell checkers can let through sum miss takes! Pay attention to details such as consistent page numbering and clear layout, well-presented illustrative material (tables, charts, etc), accurate and consistent system for references, table of contents and so on.

How to assess progress

See assessment criteria suggested in ▶ **[W16]** *Marking your written performance.*

W16 | Marking your written performance

W16

How to use this questionnaire

The questionnaire is divided into a series of key points (on the left-hand side). Each key point represents one aspect of performance that may or may not be relevant in your case:

1   Read the key point and decide whether it is relevant (tick 'yes') or not (tick 'no').

2   If it is not relevant, ignore the questions under this key point and move on to the next one.

3   If the key point is relevant, answer the question(s) next to it. Make sure you also tick off the boxes on the left of each question that you answered. Then proceed to the next key point and continue in the same way

NOTE: You may put a tick between two boxes if you hesitate between two descriptions. Use 'half points' for those replies when you calculate the final score.

▼ KEY POINT

Did you have to perform within a given word limit?	YES / NO

▶ ☐ **1   How closely did you stick to the word limit?**

About twice as long/half as long as the limit (or) even more/less than that.	☐	[0]
About 1/4 longer or shorter than the word limit.	☐	[1]
About 15% over/below the word limit.	☐	[2]
Just within the word limit.	☐	[3]

Was the content of your text expected to be interesting, relevant or original?	YES / NO

▶ ☐ **2   Put yourself in the shoes of your intended (or imaginary) reader, and examine critically what you wrote. How interesting/relevant/original would s/he find it?**

Not interesting/relevant/original at all	☐	[0]
Interesting/relevant/original enough, though hardly gripping	☐	[1]
Quite interesting/relevant/original at times	☐	[2]
Very interesting/relevant/original troughout	☐	[3]

Were you set (or did you set yourself) a list of points that had to be covered in the task?	YES / NO

▶ ☐ **3   Did you manage to get all the points across somehow, or did you cover only part of them?**

Less than half	☐	[0]
About half	☐	[1]
More than half	☐	[2]
All of them	☐	[3]

Were you expected to produce a well-structured account/argument/story?

YES

NO

▶ ☐ **4** **Look at the logical structure of your text. How clear and well-balanced is it?**

No real structure, ideas just occurred at the time	☐ [0]
The structure is not very obvious (or) there is some lack of balance between different parts of the argument/presentation	☐ [1]
Good balance and logical structure, very easy to follow	☐ [2]
Elegantly structured with perfectly clear, logical and well-balanced ideas	☐ [3]

▼

Were you meant to produce a piece of fluent, well connected text?

YES

NO

▶ ☐ **5** **Read it aloud. If the text is several pages long, read only one page. Does it read well?** *Tick one answer:*

Sentences are not connected together and may be incomplete. Reads like a telegram.	☐ [0]
There are frequent problems related to sentences that may be too short (or) too long (or) awkwardly connected.	☐ [1]
Reads quite well overall, but reading the text aloud shows up one or two clumsy passages.	☐ [2]
Good use of sentence structure and punctuation make it easy to read aloud. It sounds 'right' throughout.	☐ [3]

▼

Were you supposed to follow the conventions of a particular text type (e.g. formal letter, academic paper, report, etc)?

YES

NO

▶ ☐ **6** **Take a critical look at your text in terms of what is normally expected in a text of this type (style conventions, type of language used, layout, quality of presentation, referencing, headings, opening and closing phrases, etc). Remember that even colloquial genres have their own set of conventions! How does your text comply with the relevant conventions?**

I didn't really think about it (or) I just don't know the conventions	☐ [0]
There are some things I am not quite sure about	☐ [1]
My text complies with the conventions as far as I know	☐ [2]
I am pretty confident that my text complies in all respects	☐ [3]

▼

Do you normally experience some lack confidence or anxiety with writing tasks?

YES

NO

▶ ☐ **7** **How did you cope with the task this time?**

It was all a real struggle	☐ [0]
Most of it was hard work	☐ [1]
Most of it was reasonably manageable	☐ [2]
It was all very manageable	☐ [3]

▼

Did you use a dictionary to look up new words?	YES / NO

▶ ☐ **8** Look away from your text. Now try to list from memory all the words that you looked up in the foreign language. What proportion can you remember?

I can't remember any of the words I looked up	☐	[0]
I have forgotten at least half the words I looked up	☐	[1]
I can remember most of the words I looked up	☐	[2]
I can remember all the words I looked up	☐	[3]

Did you try to complete the task without looking up words in the dictionary or other reference material?	YES / NO

▶ ☐ **9** What type of words did you use?

Even the simplest vocabulary that I am supposed to know by now wouldn't come to my mind.	☐	[0]
I used only very basic vocabulary that I have known for a while.	☐	[1]
I used mostly basic vocabulary, with one or two attempts to use more sophisticated terms (for my present level) or recently learnt words.	☐	[2]
I consistently tried to use sophisticated vocabulary (for my level) and recently learnt words.	☐	[3]

Was language accuracy relevant in this task?	YES / NO

▶ ☐ **10** Examine your text as closely as you can, including any revisions made as you were writing it. If you haven't done it already, use any means available (dictionaries, grammar, other people, etc) to check the accuracy of your final text. How would you rate it?

I had no idea then and I am still not very sure now	☐	[0]
I see now quite a few mistakes that could have been easily avoided if I had been more careful at the time	☐	[1]
I can see a couple of 'silly'/careless mistakes now, but that's all	☐	[2]
All the mistakes of which I could possibly be aware at my level were either avoided altogether or corrected straight away	☐	[3]

Was there a particular rule or grammar structure (or a group of structures/rules) that you were trying to practise?	YES / NO

▶ ☐ **11** State here what the grammar focus was:

How confident are you in using the structure(s) or rule(s) now?

I gave up using it in the end	☐	[0]
I'm still confused about this rule	☐	[1]
I think I'm beginning to understand	☐	[2]
I feel pretty confident now	☐	[3]

Are you (or will you be) monitoring your progress in this skill over a period of time?	YES NO ▼	▶ ☐ **12** Read a similar task that you wrote in the past. How would you rate your overall performance now compared to then? (If this was the first time you ever performed this kind of task, give yourself the highest score!)

I have done a lot better than this in the past! ☐ [0]

Much the same as I usually do. ☐ [1]

I notice some improvement compared to previous occasions ☐ [2]

Definitely better than I have ever done on this kind of task! ☐ [3]

Did you have a specific purpose or focus when you undertook this task?	YES NO ▼	▶ ☐ **13** State here what your main purpose was:	

Overall, how effective was this task in achieving your goal(s)?

Not effective at all in the area(s) that mattered to me, or in any other area. ☐ [0]

Possibly effective in some area(s), but not really in the area(s) that mattered to me. ☐ [1]

Some moderate success in the area(s) that mattered to me. ☐ [2]

A total success in the area(s) that mattered to me. ☐ [3]

Is there anything that has not been covered in this questionnaire and that you would like to include in the criteria?	YES NO ▼	▶ ☐ **14** State here what other point you would like to assess:	

Poor performance ☐ [0]

Modest/average performance ☐ [1]

Adequate/good performance ☐ [2]

Excellent/outstanding performance ☐ [3]

How to assess your progress

1 Add up the points that you scored (all ticked boxes on the right). Multiply your score by 100 and write the number you find as value **S** on the equation below.

2 Count the number of questions that you chose to answer (all ticked boxes on the left) and multiply that number by 3. Enter it on the equation below as value **Q**.

3 Calculate the equation for the values that you just entered. The result is your final mark, expressed as a percentage of the best possible performance.

$$\frac{S = \underline{\hspace{1.5cm}}}{Q = \underline{\hspace{1.5cm}}} = Mark = \underline{\hspace{1.5cm}} \%$$

4 Read the comments below to see what your mark indicates and how your performance could be improved.

Interpreting the results

Note: Language learning can be a slow process, so don't be surprised if your score takes a while to improve. Once you reach Band B, you may stay there for a long period of time: this simply indicates that you are making good progress, as the marking scale is designed to 'grow up' with you.

- **Band E –** *Mark = 0 to 20%:* Your performance was poor. This could be for several reasons: you may have tried something too difficult for your present level (try something a bit easier next time); you may need more guidance for the moment (try to join a course or find a helpful partner to study with); or it might just be that you were not really concentrating on the task (try harder next time!).

- **Band D –** *Mark = 21 to 40%:* There is plenty of room for improvement. Examine your answers carefully and think what you would need to do in order to improve your scores in each of the questions where your score is 1 or below. Experiment with different learning techniques for the areas and skills that need improving. For extra guidance, you can use the checklists of *'Typical problems'* provided in Chapter 5, pp39–50.

- **Band C –** *Mark = 41 to 60%:* You are working well, but you could still improve in some areas. Look especially at the questions where you scored less than 2. How could you improve those particular scores? What would you need to do in order to turn some of the two's into three's next time? Try out a few new learning techniques that you haven't tried before and see which ones seem to work best for you.

- **Band B –** *Mark = 61 to 80%:* You are doing very well. You are probably making the most of your ability right now. Try to improve even more, but don't get obsessed if you can't manage to get a higher score! So long as your mark doesn't go down overall you are on the right track. Keep experimenting too: you could for instance try to assess different aspects of your performance (answering different questions from the checklist) or start writing other types of text.

- **Band A –** *Mark = 81 to 100%:* That is an excellent result! You seem to have reached your latest learning target successfully. However, do check that you are stretching yourself enough. Extreme confidence sometimes means that a learner is living on 'old' knowledge and skills. Could this be your case? It might be time to set yourself a new, more ambitious target. Perhaps you could try to assess different aspects of your performance (answering different questions from the checklist) or start writing more challenging kinds of text.

chapter 11 Speaking

What does speaking in a foreign language involve?

For most learners, speaking in the foreign language is a key priority. Not only is speaking a vital life skill, but conversing with native speakers adds motivation in its own right, whatever one's original reason for learning the language.

Speech events

Speaking usually involves real-time interaction: in other words, not only planning and producing language at high speed, but also listening to the words and observing the reactions of those we are speaking with (our **interlocutors**). For this reason, linguists prefer to see spoken language not so much in terms of texts as in terms of **speech events**, i.e. situations where people speak and listen.

The vast majority of speech events in day-to-day life are **conversations**. These are face-to-face or telephone interactions where there is no fixed 'script' and where everyone involved has the right to join in (to **take their turn**) and to change topic if and when they wish. An example would be a chat between friends in a restaurant, or a negotiation between two business people.

Conversations take up such a large proportion of our lives that handling them is crucial in a foreign language. Unfortunately, the fact that they have no fixed script and involve a lot of listening means that conversations with native speakers can be quite daunting for beginner and elementary learners. Another fact to bear in mind is that speech events – even informal conversations – have **rules**, which can differ from language to language. The rules may determine how to open or close a conversation, for example: when phoning a friend or acquaintance in Bosnian or Arabic, say, it would be impolite not to inquire about your interlocutor's family before bringing up the real reason for ringing. Or how to take your turn: interrupting is acceptable in Spain (speakers expect to be interrupted by listeners eager to contribute), whereas in English it indicates a lack of interest in your interlocutor's message.

Other speech events are more **formalised** in character. Here, there is usually a pre-arranged topic, or even a word-for-word script, and **speaking rights** (who can speak when, and in what form) are strictly defined. In a university lecture, for example, the topic is determined by the syllabus and may even be scripted from the lecturer's notes; and the lecturer has the right to speak most or all of the time, whereas the students can only ask brief questions. Other examples of formalised speech events are job interviews, formal debates, or religious ceremonies.

Though formalised speech events take up a very small proportion of our overall talking time, the ability to cope with them is a key marker of adulthood. Here too, rules can vary from language to language: in job interviews in some countries, for example, the interviewee is expected to show his or her certificates to the panel before talking about the job. Moreover, rules of formalised events tend to be complex, and breaking them can be highly embarrassing for the speaker. Hence knowing the rules of a likely range of formalised speech events is useful for anyone who wishes to be more than a tourist in a foreign country.

There is a third, in-between category of speech events that we could call **transactions**. These usually involve one person getting information, goods or services from another: buying a ticket at a railway station, asking the way in the street, etc. They tend to be short and quite formalised, but they can potentially turn into fully-fledged conversations: for example, asking someone for a light can prompt the follow-up *Where are you from?*, which can lead into a lengthy, wide-ranging conversation.

The speaking process

Before the event

Like writing, speaking involves planning messages before and while we speak. With some formalised speech events (e.g. a presentation by a company representative), pre-planning can be very careful and thorough. With conversations, however, there may be only a general intention (e.g. to ask a friend about her holiday in Florida); and very often, the intention may be more to oil the social wheels (*Hi – what's new?*) than to get any particular message across.

While speaking

While we speak, however, a lot of short-term planning is going on – and under constant time pressure. In conversations, we need to listen to what our interlocutor is saying and use what we hear to roughly plan our response. We then have to listen out for a potential change-over point (a look, a micro-pause, a falling intonation that signals the end of a 'sentence'; or, in Spanish, a rephrasing of what has just been said) – and then to start speaking at once, before we miss our chance. When we are asked a direct question, this is fairly easy, but getting a word in edgeways between two native speakers as they hotly debate an issue is no mean feat!

The detailed planning of what we are about to say usually happens a clause at a time. While saying one clause, we get the key content words for the next from **long-term memory** (our permanent memory store) and assemble them in **working memory** (the temporary store of everything we are paying attention to right now) – e.g. to make the skeleton sequence *saw – guy – bus – yesterday*. Then we fill in the rest, to give e.g. *I saw this guy on the bus yesterday*. All this has to be done in 'real time', i.e. we cannot stop to ponder, pick up the dictionary, etc. For non-native speakers, this makes the task doubly hard. On the one hand, if we don't know a language very well, searching for words and grammar rules tends to be a slow, high-attention business. On the other hand, whereas native speakers store complex grammatical structures as ready-to-use templates (e.g. the German *Obwohl ich [X in Y] hätte sehen müssen – Although I should have seen [X in Y]*), less proficient learners have to assemble everything piece by piece. The end result of all this is often working memory overload, which means a choice of two evils: either have embarrassing silences while we search and assemble our sentences, in which case someone else may take over our turn; or search and assemble less carefully, in which case we risk making 'silly' mistakes (e.g. *Obwohl ich musste haben sehen [X in Y]*).

But skilled speakers (including all native speakers) have two ways of relieving the pressure on working memory. Firstly, they use a lot of **formulae**: prefabricated chunks of language that don't have to be searched for and assembled piece by piece (e.g. *You'll never believe [X] > You'll never believe who I saw on the bus yesterday*). Secondly, they have techniques to gain themselves thinking time. For example, using **fillers** like *know what I mean* or *sort of, like*, or repeating or what they have just said, can free up enough working memory to enable them to search for the right grammar-ending or the most tactful turn of phrase.

Pronouncing the message

Finally our brain instructs our speech organs (lungs, vocal chords, tongue, jaw, lips) to actually pronounce the clause we have assembled. But this final stage, as we all know, is no simple matter – in fact, pronunciation is the one language skill in which very few foreign learners ever become indistinguishable from native speakers.

This is probably not only a question of old (i.e. mother-tongue) physical habits dying hard. There is also a question of identity: for adults, at least, our accent shows who we are, and who we are does not change when we are abroad. For children, by contrast, 'being accepted' by others is crucial, which is a key reason why they tend to develop better accents than adults if they live in the foreign country. Similarly, those adults who wish to be accepted into the foreign community, e.g. because they marry into it, are the most likely to develop the best accent (though they also get the most practice).

Learning to speak in a foreign language

The key to successful foreign-language speaking is quite simple, in fact: lots of practice. Lack of fluency, as we have seen, happens when our planning processes are slow and attention-greedy. But the more we overload our working memory with the same things – searching for the same words and endings, piecing together the same grammatical structures – the more our brain tries to cut corners: the searches become faster and more automatic, and we start 'chunking' the phrases and structures into ready-to-use formulae and grammar templates.

What this also means is that the best practice is practice which 'stretches' us. In other words, if we don't overload our working memory a little, there's no reason for the brain to find ways of cutting corners! This means that, if we can handle speaking to classmates, we should try speaking to native speakers; and if we can handle small-talk with one native speaker, we should try discussing more complex topics or speak with a group of native speakers.

As for pronunciation, our first goal should be to become **comprehensible**. Once we have got that far, we can then ask ourselves how **native-like** we want to become – which is a question of deciding how much effort we want to put into it. A few learners are natural mimics. For those of us who aren't, plenty of intensive, focused pronunciation work – listen-and-repeat work with cassettes, for example – is needed to get through the 'fluent-but-foreign' accent barrier.

TECHNIQUES

The rest of this chapter gives a step-by-step description of all the techniques suggested for improving your speaking skills.

Arts review

S1

What is it good for?

If you like reading, going to the cinema, the theatre or listening to music, this technique will develop your ability to talk about your interest in greater depth. It is a good ice-breaker when you don't know what to talk about with a partner. (If you need writing practice, you can use the questions that are suggested here as the basic structure for a written composition based on a book, a film, a musical performance or a play that interests you.)

How to proceed

1 Think about a particular book, film, concert or play that interests you (it can be in the foreign language or in your native language).

2 Describe it to a partner (for oral practice) or write a 500-word review about it (for writing practice), covering the points listed below.

- If you are talking to a partner, ask him/her to contribute by asking you further questions or making comments throughout the conversation (this is not a speech!).

- If you don't have a partner, you may use the questions below as a basis for the ▶ **[S6]** *Imaginary chats* or ▶ **[S4]** *Recording yourself* techniques.

For films, plays and books with a plot

- What is the title and who is the author (and the director if appropriate)?
- Who are the main characters?
- Describe the personality of the main character.
- What happens in the story?
- If you had to choose a passage from the story, what would this be?
- Describe your chosen passage and explain why you chose it.

- Was there something you did not like? If so, what was it and why did you not like it?
- Overall, what made you find the book/film/play interesting or enjoyable?
- If it was a book/film/play written in the foreign language, how did you cope with the language? (Give details of your achievements and difficulties.)

For non-fiction books and TV documentaries

- What is the title and who is the author/director?
- What type of book/documentary is it?
- How did you come across it?
- What is the main topic and how is the book/documentary structured?
- What sub-topics does it go into?
- Does it have an overall 'message' or opinion?

- If you had to choose a section from the book/documentary, what would this be? Explain why.
- Was there something you did not like? If so, what was it and why did you not like it?
- Overall, what did you learn from the book/documentary?
- If it was a book/documentary in the foreign language, how did you cope with the language? (Give details of your achievements and difficulties.)

For musical performances

- What type of performance is it? (CD, live concert, etc).
- How did you come across it?
- Who composed the music and who performed it?
- Describe the music in as much detail as you can. What instruments were used?
- Describe the musicians' performance in as much detail as you can.
- If it was a live performance, describe the venue and the type of audience (otherwise, imagine what type of person would listen to this music).

- If you had to choose a piece from the performance, what would this be? Explain why.
- How does this music make you feel? If you had to represent the music through a visual image, what image would spring to mind? *(When I hear this music, I can see...)*
- Was there something you did not like? If so, what was it and why did you not like it?

---

3 If you are talking to a partner, ask him/her to tell you about a book, film, concert or play that interests him/her using the same set of questions.

S2

How to assess progress

- If you used the technique as an ice-breaker for conversation, you can regard your performance as successful so long as you and your partner have engaged in an interesting conversation about things that interest you.

- If you used the technique to improve your speaking, record yourself while you talk (▶ **[S4]** *Recording yourself*) and give yourself a mark using ▶ **[S14]** *Marking your spoken performance*.

- If you used the technique to improve your writing, give yourself a mark using ▶ **[W16]** *Marking your written performance*.

S2 | **Don't look!**

What is it good for?

When you don't see your partner, you can't use facial expressions or hand gestures to communicate. This technique forces you to convey accurate messages by means of language alone and is particularly useful as training for telephone conversations.

How to proceed

1 Suppress eye contact with your partner by...

- doing the task over the phone

- putting a screen between you (or sitting on either side of an open door).

- sitting with your backs to each other.

2 Choose (or create) a task in which there is an information gap between the speakers (i.e. one speaker needs to get information from the other speaker in order to complete the task). Here are some examples:

- Perform a role play involving a telephone conversation (▶ **[S3]** *Creating a role play*)

- Make a simple drawing (e.g. geometric figures) and describe it to your partner, who must try to draw the same picture following your directions (you may need to prepare a list of basic vocabulary beforehand).

- Find a picture showing many people (or many pictures of different people) and describe one person. Then show the picture(s) to your partner, who must figure out which person you described.

- Take an object of little value (pen, writing pad, etc) and hide it in another part of the building. Come back and give your partner precise directions so that s/he can go and find it without you. Repeat the exercise with an object hidden by your partner.

- Give your partner directions to draw your family tree. Then test the results by asking him/her specific 'who is who?' questions.

- Make two identical collections of small everyday objects (e.g. six lumps of sugar, three pencils, two books, a piece of paper and two pieces of gravel for each of the speakers). Arrange your collection of objects in a particular way on your side of the table (you can fold up the paper, cross up two pencils on top of the book, and so on). Then try to get your partner to arrange his/her collection in the same way.

Creating a role play

S3

How to assess progress

- An information gap task is successful when your partner can do the task required.

- It can be very useful to find out which of your directions or statements may have confused your partner. If you record the conversation (▶ **[S4]** *Recording Yourself*) and listen to it together, you should be able to find out what went wrong and work out how you could have made your directions less ambiguous.

What is it good for?

When planning this activity, you should choose situations in which you could expect to find yourself some day. By writing up the role cards you will be obliged to find out the type of language that you would need in that particular situation. In that way, when you actually find yourself in the real-life situation you will have a range of key words and phrases readily available in your memory.

How to proceed

Prepare two separate cue-cards (plus any other 'props') for a role play, as in the example shown below. You need to ...

1 Choose a situation in which you would like to be able to speak confidently.

2 Imagine what basic steps a typical conversation in this situation would follow.

3 Design a set of guidelines for each of the speakers involved, following your list of basic steps. Don't write full sentences that they would read out! You want them to make up the actual sentences as they speak. You could even write the guidelines in English (to prevent them from just reading out what you wrote) and provide a list of essential vocabulary and key phrases that they can use.

Make sure to create an '**information gap**' between the speakers. In other words, make sure that Speaker A doesn't already know everything that Speaker B will be saying, so that there is a genuine reason for them to talk. The best tasks are those where one speaker has to get specific information from the other.

The task is also a lot more interesting (and useful) if there is an **unexpected problem** to solve (e.g. the waiter comes back and tells you that the dish you ordered is no longer available, your client's credit card has actually expired, etc).

The example on the following page shows two role-cards and a menu for a restaurant role play.

S4

Role A Waiter	You are a waiter in a restaurant. Greet your customer and take his/her order, answering any questions as required. The chef has just informed you that potatoes have ran out and therefore no potato dishes can be served. These dishes contain potato: • Shepherd's pie • Potato and leek bake • Vegetarian moussaka • Lamb moussaka

Role B Customer	You are a customer in a restaurant. Look through the menu and find out from the waiter what options are available for you (being a vegetarian, you cannot eat anything containing meat or fish).

Menu	• Spaghetti bolognese • Shepherd's pie (with Scottish beef) • Cumberland sausages • Lamb moussaka • Creamy potato and leek bake • Vegetarian shepherd's pie • Vegetarian moussaka • Thai fish soup • Red-hot vegetarian chilli and rice • Potato and leek bake

How to assess progress

• Try acting it out yourself with a partner. Follow your guidelines very closely the first time. Then repeat the exercise asking your partner to make up some additional details. This will show you what further vocabulary you might still need.

• If you don't have a partner, perform the whole conversation yourself, using a different voice for each role (e.g. squeaky voice vs. deep voice); ▶ [S6] *Imaginary chats*.

• Record your performance if you can (▶ [S4] *Recording yourself*). Assess it (▶ [S14] *Marking your spoken performance*) and try to improve it.

S4 ## Recording yourself

What is it good for?

This is an excellent way to obtain feedback on your performance. While you are speaking, your mind is focusing on what you want to say and it is difficult (and frustrating!) to be monitoring your performance at the same time. Once it is on tape, you can look back on it (just as you do with a piece of writing) and even discuss your performance with somebody else.

How to proceed

At home: a dictaphone or a decent walkman is ideal for recording yourself if you are the only one speaking, but you may need to move the microphone from one speaker to the other if somebody else is talking. Video can provide you with more useful information as it also shows your body language. We all hate seeing ourselves struggling with a foreign language in front of a camera, but you soon get used to it and the benefits are well worth the initial embarrassment!

In a Language Centre: language learning audio stations generally have headsets with microphones. Some of them even allow you to plug in two headsets (for you and your partner). Bring a tape that is blank on both sides, and check with the technician in charge whether you will be able to play back the recording at home (recordings made on language learning stations often play backwards on domestic machines!).

How to assess progress

• Listen to the recording, focusing on the area on which you want to improve. You may also look at ▶ [S14] *Marking your spoken performance* for a list of possible criteria.

• Ask somebody else to listen to the recording with you and discuss your performance.

• Using the tape as a dictaphone, transcribe the recording and analyse it (▶ [G5] *Self-transcript*)

S5 | Tandem ice-breakers

What is it good for?

Tandem learning (i.e. teaming up with a foreign student in order to learn each other's language) is a very useful way to improve your foreign language skills. However, it is often difficult to know what to do at first, especially if one of you is only a beginner in the language. These ice-breakers should give you a few ideas.

How to proceed

Many of the techniques described in this chapter can be used as ice-breakers: If one you is a beginner, try ▶ **[S2]** *Don't look!* From elementary level upwards, you can try ▶ **[S1]** *Arts review.*

Drawing each other's family tree

This is a good way to get to know each other (see ▶ **[S2]** *Don't look!* for step-by-step directions). You could encourage conversation by giving a physical and psychological description of each of the people in the tree, including their occupations, likes and dislikes, etc. You could also tell each other what it is that you like most (or least!) in each of these people. Make sure that both of you contribute equally to the conversation.

Newspapers

1 Bring a recent newspaper from each of your countries (or download them from the Web) and go through both papers together.

2 Choose two news items that are clearly country-specific (one for each country). The native speaker will try to explain the background of his/her news item to the non-native speaker.

3 Then scan the papers again, this time looking for issues or stories that you both know about (preferably ones in which you are both interested as well!). Select two of these (one from each paper) and discuss your opinions together.

Net searches

A similar technique could be used with Web searches if you have access to the Internet. Search for the word 'Association' in your target language. The list that you will obtain is likely to include all sorts of completely different types of associations in the country. Choose a few of them from each country, and work out together what type of people are members and what the aims of the association are. Unless one of you is looking for a specific type of association in the other country, you can just go on exploring at your leisure, so long as what you see on the screen keeps you both interested and talking. If the conversation dries up, go back to the list of associations and start again from another entry.

Comparing cultures

You will always find something to talk about if you start comparing aspects of your two cultures. Here are just a few ideas:

• **Food and drink:** explain to each other what people eat at different times of the day in your country. If appropriate, describe how diet changes from one season to another throughout the year. What do men, women and children normally drink in your country? What would be the options for a vegetarian? For a meat eater? For a person on a low-fat diet? What is the national dish? What is your favourite dish? If you want to give more language focus to the task, tell your partner how to prepare a particular dish from your country.

• **Social issues:** explain to your partner how the different generations get on with each other in your country and try to give reasons for the situations that you describe. Describe how the rich, the middle class, the working class and the poor are divided. How does the country compare to the city? What roles do men and women play in society?

• **Regional clichés**: using a map of your country, go through each region explaining what the rest of the country says about the people from that region, and any other things for which the region is known. Try to find equivalences between both countries.

• **National clichés**: tell your partner two good things and two bad things that people in your country say about people in his/her country. Allow your partner to react and ask him/her to justify his/her views with specific examples. Swap around and repeat the exercise.

• **Children's' games**: describe to each other the games that children play in your country. Try to include both indoor and outdoor games. You may also teach each other any phrases or rhymes that children normally say or sing while playing some of those games. Try to find the names of similar games in both languages. Find a simple game that you can play together where you are and play it, using the relevant language (pre-teach each other any key words needed, e.g. *Your throw, Don't cheat, I won, Pass*, etc).

How to assess progress

As the aim of these tasks is only to break the ice, you can say that you have been successful if you got to know each other a bit better and some of the initial embarrassment has vanished. If this did not happen, try a different ice-breaker next time. Once you both feel comfortable, try to give some focus to your meetings and to use each other for activities that are directly related to your actual language learning needs.

Imaginary chats

What is it good for?

As discussed in 'What does speaking in a foreign language involve?' (p118), speaking is a highly complex skill that requires sophisticated levels of mental processing. This technique helps you automatise the process. You can use it at two different levels:

1   Making whole sentences that you can 'hear' in your head (though this only practices the mental part of the speaking process).

2   Actually talking aloud (even in a whisper). If you are on your own, this is far better, as it activates all the processes involved in speech production.

How to proceed

When you have nothing special to do (while walking in the street, etc), talk to yourself in the foreign language. You can do this even if you are a beginner. Here are a few very simple tasks that you can try:

If you are a beginner

1   Introduce yourself (name, occupation, where you live, where you come from, what you like/dislike, etc). Try to say as much as you can. Then talk about somebody else using the third person.

2   Pick out any sign in the street and spell out every word in it (naming letters in the foreign language!).

3   Look around, pick out a person at random and describe him/her (physical appearance, clothing, and your guesses about his/her character, occupation, likes and dislikes, etc)

4   When you go shopping, try to mentally say all the prices in the foreign language (choose a shop with expensive three-figure items).

5   If you are feeling bored in a waiting room, describe the room and the furniture in it, saying how everything is arranged.

6   As you are going from A to B, explain how to get there in the foreign language. Use different forms of address depending on who is your imaginary interlocutor at the time.

For non-beginners, there are even more topics

7   Imagine that somebody is with you and talk about anything you like (e.g. the latest gossip or a recent piece of news, etc).

8   Alternatively, you could simply 'think out loud' (or 'talk' mentally if there are people around).

9   Another useful exercise is to describe everyday actions step by step while you are performing them. For instance: *I go down the stairs, open the front door and look for a milk bottle on my doorstep. There is no milk bottle: the milkman is late again. I go back inside, take the kettle, turn the tap and fill the kettle. While the water is boiling I take a cereal bowl…* (and so on).

10   Many people talk to themselves while they are solving a problem (e.g. sorting documents such as course notes, bank statements or computer files; fitting a plug; deciding in what order to do a series of jobs, etc). Try to do this in the foreign language.

How to assess progress

*   If you are happy with a **subjective approach,** just ask yourself (a) whether you actually managed to complete the task that you had set yourself (you could set yourself a target such as *I shall talk to myself for ten minutes without reverting to my mother tongue*); (b) how frequently you got stuck or reverted to your own language; and (c) whether you feel that your fluency is improving and that you are beginning to 'think' in the foreign language.

*   A more **objective approach** would involve recording your performance (▶ [S4] *Recording yourself*) and applying the techniques used in ▶ [S14] *Marking your spoken performance*. If you want to put an accurate figure on your level of fluency, write a transcript of the recording (▶ [G5] *Self-transcript*), count the words in it, time the recording and measure your fluency in words-per-minute. Repeat a few weeks later and measure the improvement.

S7 | Learning a song

What is it good for?

This technique offers the same benefits as the techniques used in ▶ **[G8]** *Learn it by heart,* only it is more enjoyable and can be more motivating, especially if you like music. Music will also make the words easier to remember and the musical line may guide you naturally into the correct intonation and stress patterns of the language.

How to proceed

1   Get a recording of a song.

2   If you don't have a copy of the lyrics, try to transcribe them yourself (▶ **[L7]** *Writing a transcript*).

3   If you feel that the language is at a level that you can roughly understand, try to translate the lyrics yourself, otherwise seek help from a competent speaker. It is not essential to understand every single word, but it will make the song easier to remember and you will also learn more.

4   If you can, get a proficient speaker to read out the lyrics one line at a time and record them, so that you can use the ▶ **[S10]** *Listen and repeat* technique.

5   Read out the lyrics slowly. Take one line at a time and repeat it (without singing) several times, faster and faster until you can match the tempo used in the song. Then move on to the next line. It will help you if you give each syllable the same length as in the song (beat the rhythm with your hand to feel the stresses).

6   Once you can speak the lyrics at the right speed, start singing to the music until you are able to fit in all the lyrics without difficulty.

7   Learn the lyrics, one verse at a time.

8   Sing the song again from memory at regular intervals until you don't need to check the lyrics any more.

How to assess progress

You have succeeded when you can sing the song. Being able to sing a few songs is a very useful life-skill at parties, on coach trips, etc in a foreign country. It is also a quick way to gain a lot of credit from native speakers!

S8 | Interrupting your partner

What is it good for?

Even at advanced levels, turn-taking skills are difficult to pick up. Every culture has its unwritten rules regarding what is the polite way to take turns in a conversation. Some cultures rely on interruption as a sign of interest in what your partner is saying, while in others, even a very subtle stress error in your turn-taking sentence can make you sound rude. This technique provides practice in such vital skills. You may find it useful to analyse native speakers' turn-taking strategies (▶ **[L6]** *Observing native speakers*) before you tackle this exercise.

How to proceed

1   Find a partner whose level of proficiency is at least similar to your own (if your level is advanced, it is best to team up with a native speaker).

2   Prepare to record your performance (▶ **[S4]** *Recording yourself*)

3   Choose a topic in which you are both interested (see ▶ **[S5]** *Tandem ice-breakers* for ideas).

4   Set yourself a precise time limit (between five and fifteen minutes), and state how many times you expect to interrupt your partner during that time (e.g. four times in five minutes).

5   Turn on the recorder and start talking. Try to interrupt as many times as possible without being rude at any time.

6   As soon as you reach the time limit, switch off the recorder.

How to assess progress

1   Listen to the recording again and count the number of interruptions. Give yourself 50% if you have met your set target, plus 10% for each additional interruption (or take off marks in the same way if you are below the target).

2   To fine-tune your skills, listen to each interruption, asking yourself the following questions (you may also seek feedback from your partner):

   • Did you use a range of turn-taking strategies or always the same one?

   • Was the intonation entirely appropriate every time?

3   Repeat the exercise, trying to improve your performance (with attention to both quantity and quality) and assess your progress.

Outspeaking your partner

S9

What is it good for?

This technique will encourage you to take greater part in conversations in the foreign language. Talking to native speakers can be particularly intimidating: they can think in their own language a lot faster than you, especially if you feel self-conscious about your mistakes. By measuring your exact contribution to the conversation, this technique will help you monitor your progress and grade your targets realistically.

How to proceed

You may find it easier to try out the technique with another learner first. After that, you can repeat it with more proficient speakers until you feel ready to work with a native speaker.

1 Choose a topic in which you are both interested. You may take a recent item from the news, a common hobby, etc (you can find other ideas in ▶ [S5] *Tandem ice-breakers*).

2 Decide how much you plan to contribute to the conversation (e.g. at least 40% of what is said should be your contribution, while the remaining 60% can be your partner's).

3 Set up a tape-recorder and record your conversation (it should last no more than five minutes). During the conversation, try to take as much part as you can. The idea is that you should speak as much as you committed yourself to do. Your partner should not try to help you any more than he/she would in a polite real-life conversation.

How to assess progress

• Using a stop-watch, listen to the tape and time your own contribution to the conversation. However this will not be a reliable measure if your partner speaks significantly faster than you (see alternative method below).

• Count the words you said:

1 In your own time, listen to the tape and transcribe everything that was said using a word-processor. You are likely to spot some language mistakes in your contribution, and you may want to check the grammar and correct the mistakes as you go. Even though it is not the main point of the exercise, it can be a useful writing exercise (do not *add* words, though!).

2 Once you have the whole transcript, cut and paste all the sentences that you said into a separate file and do a word count on it (most word-processors have a word-counting facility). Do another word count on your partner's sentences.

• Your contribution should represent a percentage similar to the figure that you set yourself as a target before the conversation.

• Repeat the exercise a few days later with the same speaker, raising the target by 10% or more as required. Alternatively, you can keep the same target, but talk to somebody who is more proficient or talkative than your previous partner.

S10 | Listen and repeat

What is it good for?

This is a classic exercise to improve pronunciation. If you follow it up with ▶ **[G8]** *Learn it by heart*, you will also increase your vocabulary and help the processing of grammar become more automatic when you speak.

How to proceed

1 Take a recording that you can understand (e.g. from a course book). You may prefer to use one that has a written transcript that you can read out, or even write it yourself beforehand (▶ **[L7]** *Writing a transcript*).

2 Play the first sentence in the recording and stop the tape.

3 Repeat the sentence you just heard, trying to copy the speaker as closely as possible.

4 Play the next sentence and continue in the same way until the end of the recording.

How to assess progress

- The simplest way is to replay the sentence immediately after you repeat it.

- If you have two machines (one player and one recorder), you can record yourself and compare the two recordings. If you are working in a Language Centre, some of the recordings available may contain gaps that enable you to record yourself on a special student track. On language learning machines you can do this over and over again without erasing the master track.

- Of course, the best source of feedback is a native or highly proficient speaker.

S11 | Pronunciation drills

What is it good for?

Pronunciation drills are a quick and easy way to familiarise your speech organs with the new positions they need to take in the foreign language, just like gymnastics. Here you are also encouraged to analyse the language for yourself and to focus on your own problem areas by creating the drill yourself.

How to proceed

1 You will probably know which sounds are causing you problems. If you are not sure, ask a competent speaker to help you draw up a list of priorities (no more than three or four sounds at a time). There are three typical kinds of problem:
   a You just can't get your mouth to pronounce a particular sound.
   b You can't make the difference between two (or more) sounds that seem very similar to you.
   c You put stresses in the wrong places.

2 Prepare the material for your drill depending on your type of problem:
   a A list of words or sentences containing the sound in question..
   b Pairs of words (e.g. 'sheep' vs. 'ship') or sentences contrasting the sounds (e.g. 'sixty sheep were skipping in the field').
   c A list of words (or sentences) with the same stress pattern.

3 To make the drill more fun, you could choose your words or sentences so that they are related to a particular topic, or make up a whole story with them. Putting them in context will also make them easier to remember.

4 Check with a proficient speaker that every word or sentence in your list is pronounced as you believe it is (this is important as you are about to create a habit that could be very difficult to change afterwards). If you can, ask your helper to read out the drill for you and record it.

5 Read out the drill and record yourself (▶ **[S4]** *Recording yourself*), or use the ▶ **[S10]** *Listen and repeat* technique if you have a model on tape.

How to assess results

- If you are working with a proficient speaker to help you, simply ask him/her to correct you immediately each time you make an error until you can pronounce the sounds correctly.

- If you are working alone, it is essential that you record yourself, as you will hear your accent much better (it is very common to realise just how 'foreign' you sound only when you hear yourself on tape).

S12 | Reading aloud

What is it good for?

This is a tried and tested way to improve your pronunciation. You may find that it helps you build confidence in you own accent and become more fluent when you speak. It is also a useful real-life skill. However, remember that rhythm and intonation when reading out loud is very different from that of natural speech. It is also difficult to get information from a text while you are reading out loud, so read it through silently first.

How to proceed

1   Find a text that you can understand. It should not be too long (about half a page at most). Check its full meaning (▶ [R6] *Intensive reading)* before you start reading it aloud.

2   If you have an audio recording of the text, you can prepare this exercise using ▶ [S10] *Listen and repeat.*

3   Annotate the text as necessary to make your reading easier: highlight the sounds that cause you problems, put a vertical bar between phrases and a double vertical bar as a reminder to take a breath before a long sentence, etc.

4   Read out the text several times, until you are satisfied with your pace and pronunciation. Most people think they read out loud too slowly. This is rarely the problem: in fact, most people read out loud too quickly, so concentrate on getting a steady, unhurried rhythm.

5   Record yourself if you can (▶ [S4] *Recording yourself).* This will help you understand what particular areas need your attention (e.g. people who read too fast or forget to breathe don't notice this *while* they are reading!).

How to assess progress

Listen to the tape again and assess your performance (if you can, try to get a native speaker or another learner to do it too).

*   If your goal is good reading out loud technique, repeat Steps 4 and 5 until you are clear and comprehensible.

*   If your goal is to improve your pronunciation, repeat Steps 3 and 4. It may help if you focus on a limited number of sounds that cause you problems: highlight them on the text and check how you pronounced them in the recording.

S13 | Shadowing

What is it good for?

Shadowing is an advanced technique which consists of repeating what a speaker is saying while s/he is still talking, much like simultaneous interpreters do, but using the same language as the speaker. Processing is made more difficult by the fact that you need to use both listening and speaking skills simultaneously and under constant time pressure. By forcing your brain to work under such pressure, you are preparing it to cope with the time pressure that it has to face in real life listening and speaking. Try this if you already have a high level of proficiency; otherwise ▶ [S10] *Listen and repeat* may be a better option.

How to proceed

1   Choose a recording that you can understand and is neither too fast nor too long (about 30 seconds at first, getting longer as you get used to the task).

2   Start off with ▶ [S10] *Listen and repeat* as a warm-up (but do not read from a transcript).

3   Now play the recording without interruption, and try to repeat the speakers' words while the tape is running. You will need to adjust your pace to the pace of the speaker. If you lose track, don't stop the tape: just carry on from where you are.

4   Repeat the exercise until you are able to shadow the speaker through the whole recording.

5   To make the exercise more difficult next time, you can choose a faster speaker, or increase the duration of the recording, or skip Step 2.

6   **Simultaneous interpreting**: If you feel really confident (e.g. 'almost' native), you can try to translate what is being said into English, instead of repeating it in the foreign language. This is extremely difficult to do without stopping the tape, so don't expect miraculous results. Just follow the advice given for Step 3 above.

How to assess progress

*   The obvious criterion for success is whether or not you actually manage to reach the end of the recording without interruption. Over a period of time, you can measure your progress by noting how you have given yourself steadily harder texts to shadow (see Step 5 above).

*   At home, you could play the original recording through walkman headphones while recording yourself on a dictaphone. You can then listen to what you said and check whether it makes sense or not. In a Language Centre, you may be able to record your voice on the same tape as the speaker's, using a separate track (to hear yourself alone, just turn the *Master* volume right down and turn up the *Student* volume on your machine).

S14 | Marking your spoken performance

S14

How to use this questionnaire

The questionnaire is divided into a series of key points (on the left-hand side). Each key point represents one aspect of performance that may or may not be relevant in your case:

1 Read the key point and decide whether it is relevant (tick 'yes') or not (tick 'no').

2 If it is not relevant, ignore the questions under this key point and move on to the next one.

3 If the key point is relevant, answer the question(s) next to it. Make sure you also tick off the boxes on the left of each question that you answered. Then proceed to the next key point and continue in the same way

NOTE: You may put a tick between two boxes if you hesitate between two descriptions. Use 'half points' for those replies when you calculate the final score.

▼ KEY POINT

Key point		Question
Were good accent and intonation relevant in this task?	YES / NO	▶ ☐ **1** **Listen to your accent. How good is your pronunciation? (don't pay attention to how fast or slowly you speak for now). Tick one answer:** It doesn't sound right at all ☐ [0] A few sounds bother me ☐ [1] Still 'foreign', but quite acceptable ☐ [2] I like my accent! ☐ [3]
Was fluency relevant in this task?	YES / NO	▶ ☐ **2** **How often did you have to stop talking for a moment because you could't find a word or produce a sentence?** I had to stop and think virtually at every word ☐ [0] I had to stop fairly often, sometimes for quite a while ☐ [1] Noticeable delays were only occasional and never too long ☐ [2] I only stopped when I didn't know what to say ☐ [3]
Was there somebody else talking (as in a conversation, a group discussion or a role play)?	YES / NO	▶ ☐ **3** **How much initiative did you take in the conversation?** Not much at all, even when prompted by direct questions ☐ [0] I would only speak when I was asked a direct question ☐ [1] I took the leading role at times ☐ [2] I led the conversation most of the time ☐ [3]

Was the content of your message expected to be interesting, relevant or original? **YES** / **NO** ▼	▶ ☐ **4** **Put yourself in the shoes of your interlocutor (or a member of the audience), and listen critically to what you said. How interesting/relevant/original would s/he find it?**

Not interesting/relevant/original at all ☐ [0]

Interesting/relevant/original enough, though hardly gripping ☐ [1]

Quite interesting/relevant/original at times ☐ [2]

Very interesting/relevant/original throughout ☐ [3]

Did you intend to get the message across without using anything but the target language? **YES** / **NO** ▼	▶ ☐ **5** **Whenever you had problems (e.g. couldn't find a word, didn't understand your partner or couldn't make yourself understood), what did you do? If this happened more than once, tick off your *most typical* behaviour during this task.**

I said it in English (or) I waited for somebody to change topic ☐ [0]

I gave up and moved on to something else (or) I used gestures ☐ [1]

I opted for a less ambitious option, giving up the finer nuances ☐ [2]

I never had problems (or) I found/got my interlocutor to find another way to say the same thing ☐ [3]

Were you set (or did you set yourself) a list of points that had to be covered in the task? **YES** / **NO** ▼	▶ ☐ **6** **Did you manage to get all the points across somehow, or did you cover only part of them?**

Less than half ☐ [0]

About half ☐ [1]

More than half ☐ [2]

All of them ☐ [3]

Were you expected to produce a well-structured argument or presentation? **YES** / **NO** ▼	▶ ☐ **7** **Look at the logical structure of your presentation/ contribution. How clear and well-balanced is it?**

No real structure, ideas just occurred at the time ☐ [0]

The structure is not very obvious (or) there is some lack of balance between different parts of the argument/presentation ☐ [1]

Good balance and logical structure, very easy to follow ☐ [2]

Elegantly structured with perfectly clear, logical and well-balanced ideas ☐ [3]

| Was it important to look and sound 'in control'? | YES / NO | ▶ ☐ **8** | **Listen to the tone of your voice. Is it convincing enough for this situation?** |

		Barely audible (or) over-assertive (or) so loud it sounds rude	☐ [0]
		Not very convincing (or) a bit too quiet/a bit too loud	☐ [1]
		The tone is reasonably loud and convincing	☐ [2]
		The tone is just right: very clear and convincing	☐ [3]

☐ **9** **How much 'in control' did you feel while performing the task?** If you have a video of your performance: **look at your body language (eye contact with the audience, use of movement and gestures, etc). Do you seem in control?**

Extremely nervous/insecure. Lost control at times (e.g. went blank, got stuck, blushed noticeably, etc). ☐ [0]

Quite nervous/insecure, not very comfortable, felt/looked at the verge of losing control. ☐ [1]

Occasionally a little bit nervous/insecure, but managed to keep in control throughout the task. ☐ [2]

Totally in control, looking/feeling comfortable (or) professional. ☐ [3]

| Did you have to perform within a given time limit? | YES / NO | ▶ ☐ **10** | **How closely did you stick to the time limit?** |

About twice as long/half as long as the limit (or) even more/less than that. ☐ [0]

About 1/4 longer or shorter than the time limit. ☐ [1]

About 10% over/below the time limit. ☐ [2]

Just within the time limit. ☐ [3]

| Was it your goal to use a good range of vocabulary? | YES / NO | ▶ ☐ **11** | **What type of words did you use?** |

Even the simplest vocabulary that I am supposed to know by now wouldn't come to my mind. ☐ [0]

I used only very basic vocabulary that I have known for a while. ☐ [1]

I used mostly basic vocabulary, with one or two attempts to use more sophisticated terms (for my present level) or recently learnt words. ☐ [2]

I consistently tried to use sophisticated vocabulary (for my level) and recently learnt words. ☐ [3]

Was language accuracy relevant in this task?	YES
	NO

▶ ☐ **12** To answer questions 12 and 13, you may find it useful to record your performance, or better still: to write a word-for-word transcript of what you said. **Listen to the recording, watching out for mistakes. How many can you see in your performance?**

I didn't really know how to say anything properly.	☐	[0]
A lot of mistakes, and even now I wouldn't know how to say those things properly	☐	[1]
Quite a few, but they were mostly 'silly'/ careless mistakes.	☐	[2]
Only a few 'silly'/careless mistakes.	☐	[3]

13 **How often did you notice that you had made a mistake and corrected it straight away?**

If I ever did correct myself, I was never sure which option was right anyway.	☐	[0]
I noticed my mistakes and corrected them a couple of times	☐	[1]
I often noticed my mistakes, but I can see a few more now	☐	[2]
I corrected virtually all the mistakes that I am able to see now	☐	[3]

Are you (or will you be) monitoring your progress in this skill over a period of time?	YES
	NO

▶ ☐ **14** **Listen to a similar task recorded in the past (or just try to remember it). How would you rate your overall performance now compared to then? (If this was the first time you ever performed this kind of task, give yourself the highest score!)**

I have done a lot better than this in the past!	☐	[0]
Much the same as I usually do.	☐	[1]
I notice some improvement compared to previous occasions	☐	[2]
Definitely better than I have ever done on this kind of task!	☐	[3]

Did you have a specific purpose or focus when you undertook this task?	YES	▶ □ **15**	State here what your main purpose was:	
	NO ▼			

Overall, how effective was this task in achieving your goal(s)?

Not effective at all in the area(s) that mattered to me, or in any other area.	□	[0]
Possibly effective in some area(s), but not really in the area(s) that mattered to me.	□	[1]
Some moderate succes in the area(s) that mattered to me.	□	[2]
A total success in the area(s) that mattered to me.	□	[3]

Is there anything that has not been covered in this questionnaire and that you would like to include in the criteria?	YES	▶ □ **16**	State here what other point you would like to assess:	
	NO ▼			

Poor performance	□	[0]
Modest/average performance	□	[1]
Adequate/good performance	□	[2]
Excellent/outstanding performance	□	[3]

How to assess your progress

1 Add up the points that you scored (all ticked boxes on the right). Multiply your score by 100 and write the number you find as value S on the equation below.

2 Count the number of questions that you chose to answer (all ticked boxes on the left) and multiply that number by 3. Enter it on the equation below as value Q.

3 Calculate the equation for the values that you just entered. The result is your final mark, expressed as a percentage of the best possible performance.

$$\frac{S = \rule{2cm}{0.4pt}}{Q = \rule{2cm}{0.4pt}} = \text{Mark} = \rule{2cm}{0.4pt} \%$$

4 Read the comments below to see what your mark indicates and how your performance could be improved.

Interpreting the results

Note: Language learning can be a slow process, so don't be surprised if your score takes a while to improve. Once you reach Band B, you may stay there for a long period of time: this simply indicates that you are making good progress, as the marking scale is designed to 'grow up' with you.

- **Band E** – *Mark = 0 to 20%:* Your performance was poor. This could be for several reasons: you may have tried something too difficult for your present level (try something a bit easier next time); you may need more guidance for the moment (try to join a course or find a helpful partner to study with); or it might just be that you were not really concentrating on the task (try harder next time!).

- **Band D – *Mark = 21 to 40%:*** There is plenty of room for improvement. Examine your answers carefully and think what you would need to do in order to improve your scores in each of the questions where your score is 1 or below. Experiment with different learning techniques for the areas and skills that need improving. For extra guidance, you can use the checklists of *'Typical problems'* provided in Chapter 5, pp39–50.

- **Band C – *Mark = 41 to 60%:*** You are working well, but you could still improve in some areas. Look especially at the questions where you scored less than 2. How could you improve those particular scores? What would you need to do in order to turn some of the two's into three's next time? Try out a few new learning techniques that you haven't tried before and see which ones seem to work best for you.

- **Band B – *Mark = 61 to 80%:*** You are doing very well. You are probably making the most of your ability right now. Try to improve even more, but don't get obsessed if you can't manage to get a higher score! So long as your mark doesn't go down overall you are on the right track. Keep experimenting too: you could for instance try to assess different aspects of your performance (answering different questions from the checklist) or try out different types of speaking activities.

- **Band A – *Mark = 81 to 100%:*** That is an excellent result! You seem to have reached your latest learning target successfully. However, do check that you are stretching yourself enough. Extreme confidence sometimes means that a learner is living on 'old' knowledge and skills. Could this be your case? It might be time to set yourself a new, more ambitious target. Perhaps you could try to assess different aspects of your performance (answering different questions from the checklist) or start working on more challenging kinds of speaking activities.

Alphabetical list of DIY techniques